Frans Cronje

A TIME TRAVELLER'S GUIDE TO
SOUTH AFRICA
IN 2030

TAFELBERG

Tafelberg
An imprint of NB Publishers, a Division of Media24 Boeke (Pty) Ltd
40 Heerengracht, Cape Town
www.tafelberg.com
Text © Frans Cronje (2017)

Cover design: Simon Richardson
Book design: Nazli Jacobs
Editing: Russell Martin
Proofreading: Sean Fraser
Index: Sanet le Roux

Printed in South Africa

ISBN: 978-0-624-08250-7 (Second edition, first impression 2017)
ISBN: 978-0-624-08058-9 (First edition, first impression 2017)
ISBN: 978-0-624-08059-6 (epub)
ISBN: 978-0-624-08060-2 (mobi)

"For now we see through a glass, darkly; but then face to face: now I know in part; but then shall I know even as I am known. And now stays faith, hope, charity, these three; but the greatest of these is charity."

1 Corinthians 13: 12-13

Contents

Foreword

Nobody can predict precisely the way the future is going to play out in the long term. That is why it is much better to be vaguely right than precisely wrong. Scenario planning is a methodology that accepts this principle by identifying the forces or trends that are shaping the future, choosing the ones that are likely to have the most impact, constructing scenarios that illustrate the possible causal chains flowing from those forces or trends, and deciding on the 'flags' that will give a feel for which scenario is likely to materialise during the period under review.

In his second book, Frans Cronje has used the technique in a masterful manner to examine the plausible scenarios for South Africa to 2030. He feels this is an appropriate moment to do so as South Africa has entered the period of the Fourth Transition, the previous ones being in 1910, 1948 and 1994. He points to all the good things that have happened since 1994 under the new dispensation, but shows convincingly that we face unprecedented economic challenges as a result of the poor performance displayed by the South African economy since 2007.

In short, South Africa is at a tipping point where small random events can have a major effect on the system as a whole because of all the feedback loops contained in the system reinforcing one another and producing extreme results. In the world at large, we had two remarkable examples of this phenomenon in 2016 in the unexpected decision by Britain to leave the European Union after a referendum there, and the election of Donald Trump as the next American President when the polls were completely against him winning. Indeed, Frans begins his book with the story of how the decision of a young man named Mohamed Bouazizi to set himself alight in Tunisia in December 2010 had massive consequences for the Middle East as a whole.

Here in South Africa we have the growing frustrations of young people who have no prospect of improving their lives as the potential spark for economic and political destabilisation. Bouazizi felt exactly the same way before he died. It is therefore no surprise that Frans and his team have chosen whether popular expectations are met or remain unmet as one of the axes of the scenario matrix providing the four possible scenarios of South Africa's future to 2030. The other axis is whether the state will be dominant or weak.

The four scenarios, which all make for gripping reading, are then described in the following order. 'The Rise of the Right' scenario depicts a new model of authoritarian capitalism that sees the erosion of democratic rights and freedoms, but on the other hand a great improvement in the material conditions of almost all South Africans. This promotes a new sense of common purpose and cohesion among citizenry and propels South Africa once again to being Africa's leading economy, with its success being heralded across the emerging world. Similarities with the recent evolution of China, South Korea and Singapore come to mind.

In the second scenario, called 'The Tyranny of the Left', stagnant and negative economic growth rates persist with the state pursuing reckless out-of-date socialist policies that lead to a series of ratings downgrades and major capital flight. Inflation, debt and interest rates soar, causing widespread dejection among the public, who remain cowed and resigned to their fate. The difference between Russia and China's economic trajectory since 1978 illustrates the parting of the ways between the first and second scenarios.

The third scenario, 'The Break-up of South Africa', portrays a weak and divided government in which fragmentation, factionalism and confusion reign. Two classes of South Africans become apparent: the one within the walls, and the one outside the walls. They have very little to do with each other. Race as well as ethnic divisions deepen and it is unclear whether society will ever be put back together again.

The fourth and last scenario is undoubtedly the most positive one and is aptly titled 'Rise of the Rainbow'. South Africa is no longer the country in which people wait for the government to do something for them. It is one in which they will do it for themselves, and the government is there to help create the conditions for them to do so. Rather than weak government, this scenario describes the type of leadership in government that Nelson Mandela once fondly described as leading a flock of sheep from behind. South Africa, with a booming middle class, becomes an Asian Tiger without the authoritarianism inherent in 'The Rise of the Right' scenario. The rebound in the economy means that South Africans emerge from their self-imposed enclaves and live comfortably alongside one another.

Story-telling is an art that engages the emotions as well as the intellect. I sincerely hope that these scenarios enter the common vocabulary in South Africa in the same way that the 'High Road/Low Road' scenarios did in the mid-1980s. They should, because the narrative is very persuasive and has the capacity to inspire people to take the actions necessary to fulfil this country's extraordinary potential.

CLEM SUNTER

Chapter 1: The fourth transition

This story starts on 17 December 2010 when a young man called Mohamed Bouazizi changed the trajectory of the world forever. Mohamed was a hawker who supported his family by selling fruit and vegetables in a small town called Sidi Bouzid in rural Tunisia. Mohamed had grown up in a poor family. His father was a construction worker who had died when Mohamed was very young. According to a friend, he was a popular young man who, in addition to funding his sisters' education, was looking to buy a second-hand pick-up truck to expand his vegetable business.

At 11.30 a.m. on the morning of 17 December 2010, Mohammed poured a can of petrol over himself outside the local governor's office in Sidi Bouzid, struck a match, and set himself alight. Eighteen days later he died in a Tunisian hospital of the burns he had suffered. The events leading up to his death were the following: he had looked for work but could not find a job, which was why he turned to hawking. As a hawker, he was continually harassed by the police for not having the right trading permits to sell his fruit and vegetables, and they had extorted money and bribes from him. On the day he set himself alight he had been forced to borrow money to buy his vegetables and so could not pay a bribe to the police. A police officer had therefore slapped him in the street, spat on him, and overturned his vegetable cart. When he went to the local government office to lay a complaint, they refused to see him. So he bought his can of petrol, and returned to that same office …

A journalist estimated that 5,000 people joined his funeral procession in the small town where he had grown up, chanting, 'We weep for you today. We will make those who caused your death weep.' And indeed they did.

As news of his desperate act spread, the protests started. Within a month they had swept across Tunisia. The police tried to control them but found that they were powerless to curb the tide of human anger and frustration. In desperation, and fearing for his life, on 14 January 2011 Tunisia's President, Zine el-Abidine Ben Ali, fled to France – that country's former colonial master. The French authorities refused to accept him and he was later granted exile in Saudi Arabia. The Tunisian government collapsed soon after his departure.

To the east and the west of the country the revolt spread. In Egypt, after two weeks of violence, President Muhammad Hosni el-Sayed Mubarak announced his resignation. He had assumed the presidency of Egypt in 1981 – just eight days after the assassination of his predecessor, Anwar Sadat. Shortly after his resignation, he was arrested with his sons and put on trial for crimes against the Egyptian people. He suffered a heart attack while being questioned by police, was convicted of corruption, and sent to prison. He died in 2015.

In Libya protests culminated in the death of the country's leader, Muammar Gaddafi. Like Mubarak, Gaddafi had run his socialist dictatorship with almost no opposition for more than 30 years. Rights activists had been jailed and tortured and opposition politics suppressed. Gaddafi was all-powerful and free to act with impunity. But the illusion of stability created by his suppression of civil rights was not sufficient to withstand the growing embitterment and unmet expectations of many Libyans. By early 2011 even his once all-powerful security services were powerless to stem the tide of public anger. Surrounded by a small company of bodyguards, Gaddafi was on the run, seeking refuge in small towns as the rebellion closed in around him. Hunted like a wild animal, he hid in a drainpipe but was caught by protesters. They beat him in the street, causing his death; one gruesome description related how his former subjects bayoneted him in the rear end – a brutal end to a brutal reign.

Less than a year after Mohamed Bouazizi's death, much of the Middle East and North Africa were engulfed in turmoil. Protests or changes of government occurred across a belt that stretched from Rabat on Morocco's east coast to Muscat on the west coast of Oman – a distance of over

4,000 miles. Sixteen countries were swept up in the turmoil, which ranged from civil wars to mass protests and multiple government overthrows.

The brutal civil war in Syria, which *The Economist* described best as a 'blood-soaked mess of wars within a war', can be traced back directly to the Tunisian uprising. So, too, can the rise of ISIS, which took advantage of the ensuing chaos to establish itself in northern Iraq and Syria. Heightened tensions between Sunni and Shia Arabs, which still threaten to cause a pan-Middle Eastern civil war, have much of their recent origin in the Arab Spring. Russia in turn exploited American intransigence over the Middle East to usurp some of the influence that the United States had previously exerted as the dominant foreign power in that region. That in turn shifted the balance of power between Russia on the one hand and the European Union and the North Atlantic Treaty Organisation (NATO) on the other.

It is amazing to think that in many respects this chain of events was started by a vegetable hawker – an otherwise unremarkable young man who grew very angry that his life's expectations were unmet and that nobody was listening. Evidently that sentiment ran deep, and his action was the spark that ignited the powder keg.

Why does this matter to us? If you live in South Africa you already suspect the answer: because the circumstances that led to Mohamed Bouazizi setting himself alight describe very closely the daily struggle of millions of poor young South Africans. Massive unemployment, an out-of-touch, arrogant and corrupt government, and a rising tide of public violence.

I work for a think tank, the IRR, which among other things advises organisations and companies about social and economic trends and how the future of South Africa is likely to unfold. In the immediate aftermath of the Tunisian uprising, we were kept very busy answering requests for information about whether South Africa could go the same way. Our answer was a qualified 'not yet', and a clear 'no' if the growing frustrations of young people were resolved. But that was more than five years ago, and in the time that has elapsed since then, tensions have increased and economic performance has weakened while the government seems even more out of touch.

Now, if we are asked whether South Africa might face massive economic and political destabilisation, our answers are more guarded. This is not to suggest that South Africa will descend into the chaos of the Middle East. To be clear from the outset, we do not think it will, and none of the scenarios that appear in this book describes worlds as violent and chaotic as what we see today in the Middle East. But political change and economic destabilisation can take many forms, and we are headed (hurtling might be a better word) towards our own unique brand of trouble.

Put differently, can there be any doubt that there is a South African Mohamed Bouazizi out there already? A smart, hardworking young man who, against the odds, is doing his best to look after his family. He probably also did not complete high school and looked for a job but could not find one, so he turned to hawking to make a living for his family. He too probably faces harassment and abuse from the police because he does not have the right permit. At night, when he goes home, he shares his stories of hardship with his peers. Around them they see the wealth and prosperity of South Africa's small middle class. In newspapers they read of how politicians continuously loot the country. On the television news they watch their elected leaders' undignified squabbling.

You can gain no better window into the hopeless frustrations of life in many poor communities than to read the story of one Daniel Mulaudzi, whose shack in Hammanskraal on the outskirts of Pretoria was demolished on the orders of the Tshwane local council, formerly under the control of the African National Congress (ANC). The demolition was ordered because he had built his shack on a piece of land owned by the council but without its permission – a point he and members of the community later disputed, explaining that a councillor had given them permission to build. Nonetheless, what happened next is a warning of how close the South African government is to setting off its own powder keg. According to a news report:

Daniel Mulaudzi, 53, said the Red Ants security company came to their area on Monday and demolished houses.

'They were wearing blue overalls. We thought they wouldn't do anything as we are legal here. They started shooting at us and demolished our shacks. We were standing and not doing anything,' he said.

Sitting on a couch where his shack once was, he told of the pain he felt as he watched people tear down his home and make off with some of his belongings. Mulaudzi said he was unemployed and did not know how he would rebuild his life.

'It's painful what they did to me. I don't even have corrugated steel to even rebuild. I'm unemployed and don't know what I will do to rebuild. I slept out in the cold because we have nowhere to go. They must return our material. They even took things from our bags. Clothes, money, even our ID books were taken,' he said.

Mulaudzi told of how he and his family spent the night out in the open. Apart from his building materials having been taken, he is now gripped by fear of losing his furniture to theft.

'We sat in front of a fire the entire night to keep warm because if we leave they will take our belongings. We have been living here for five months. They said it was legal for people to live here, which is when we moved in. We were surprised to see them removing us,' he said.[1]

My colleagues and I followed that story closely and learned that the tragedy of the evictions extended far beyond the Hammanskraal residents who lost their homes. That same night, as Daniel Mulaudzi sat around the fire, guarding his possessions, another man by the name of Sam Tshabalala was mourning the death of his brother, Elias.

Elias and Sam Tshabalala were both unemployed and had been hired as casual labourers at a rate of R150 a day by the company contracted by the Tshwane council to demolish the Hammanskraal shacks. At a point during the evictions the community turned on the casual workers. Sam

---

1   http://m.news24.com/news24/SouthAfrica/News/its-painful-what-they-did-to-me-evicted-hammanskraal-resident-20160524.

Tshabalala was amongst those who managed to escape, but his brother was caught and burned alive by the people trying to save their shacks. A later news report said that the company that had hired the Tshabalala brothers had offered to donate cabbages for his funeral.

The whole incident is an all-too-common window into the cruel brutality of life for many South Africans – the poor fighting the poor just to save their homes or to earn R150 for a day of menial work. South Africans are wrong if they think this kind of thing can continue, day after day, without it one day tearing the country to pieces. Less than a year after the events at Hammanskraal, the ANC lost its majority in Tshwane and held a series of meetings to try to understand what had gone wrong.

The IRR undertakes extensive research into both employment and unemployment matters and has always found it baffling that in some of the larger urban areas there are metropolitan police departments that have divisions tasked with driving around in trucks to confiscate the goods of hawkers who do not have the right permits. This is done in a country where the youth unemployment rate is above 50%. As well as being cruel, it is a chillingly stupid example of showering sparks onto powder kegs – desperate people just trying to survive and feed their families and their small efforts being shut down by the state. If you ask the politicians and officials who give such orders what they think they are doing, they will respond that they are establishing 'order'. The brother of former President Thabo Mbeki, Moeletsi Mbeki, described this type of idiocy best as 'children playing with a hand grenade'. Imagine the order we will have when, as he warned, 'they learn how to pull out the pin'.

Making things worse is that abuse and corruption run rampant. In one incident, the Tshwane metro police burned the stalls of hawkers. In Johannesburg, the city authorities unilaterally cancelled the trading permits of hundreds of hawkers. Some years ago a colleague tried to intervene outside the IRR offices when the police came to evict a hawker and seize his goods. For her trouble she was arrested and detained at the Hillbrow police station. We were able to raise hell and she was released.

But complain about the bad treatment you get from the government – especially if you are poor – and the chances are not very good that you will get a sympathetic hearing. On applying for a driver's licence recently, I saw licensing officials screaming abuse at a woman for standing in the wrong queue. A prominent businessman told me how he had only been able to resolve a work permit dispute when in desperation he called upon the assistance of a cabinet minister. I know of people who – after exhausting every other option – referred a Johannesburg municipal billing complaint to the President's office (which, incredibly, took up the matter). In another incident, the Minister of Home Affairs had to assist with obtaining a birth certificate. Can you imagine referring a billing complaint to 10 Downing Street for the attention of the Prime Minister? I think almost every South African can relate similar tales of a government that just does not care – yet few of them are fortunate enough to be able to call upon a cabinet minister, or the police commissioner, for help.

Because South Africans are not taken seriously by their government, they are taking their frustrations to the streets. In one example, more than ten schools were burnt down by protesters who felt that provincial officials were not taking their various grievances seriously. Trains and municipal buses are routinely torched. Protesters easily resort to throwing stones at the police. We are conditioned to seeing and even accepting these things because they happen so often and so routinely. But these are not normal actions in any country. The burning of government buildings, not to mention schools and university libraries, is self-destructive and the perpetrators should be jailed. But at the same time ask yourself this: what frustration lurks under the surface that allows such things to happen?

Don't make the mistake of thinking this sort of violence and disorder will continue to play out only in poor communities. If South Africa does not take the desperation of poor people seriously, we will get to a point where a rampaging mob will march down West Street in Sandton and set fire to the banks and the law firms. We are heading there.

Now add to the mix the fact that the economy has not shown much growth over the past four or five years while inflation and interest rates are climbing, and there can be no argument that a really dangerous cocktail is developing. Even for middle-class households it has become a challenge to make it through the month as electricity prices keep rising, fuel prices do the same, rates and taxes are increased in increments far greater than inflation, and food prices escalate. Just imagine how difficult it must be for people who live in communities that have very few jobs, where large numbers of people are laid off as the economy slows, and social grants have been unable to make ends meet. Think of the woman who has to wake up at 4 a.m. and leave her sleeping children in their shack to catch a train and then a taxi for a multi-hour commute to her job as a domestic worker that will see her return home after 8 p.m. – to clear less than R2,000 a month. In her household the elder children raise the younger ones, feed them, dress them, get them off to school … and later put them to bed. Try to put your family in that position for a moment – because if you cannot do so, you will remain incredulous about some of the conclusions that will be reached in this book. While you are at it, do the maths on how she could possibly raise her family on that R2,000.

Today, in almost every respect, key economic indicators such as growth, incomes and employment are worse in South Africa than they were in Tunisia in 2011. However, we are a more democratic society, which means that frustrated people have options other than revolution to change the country. Together with the absence of religious fundamentalism, this explains why we are likely to chart a different revolutionary route from that of the Arab Spring. In Arab Spring countries, young people had to pick up rifles because all the other avenues to political change had been closed to them. South Africans can still vote for change – which is happening. But many of the institutions critical to our future as a democracy have been undermined. This is incredibly dangerous because if avenues of democratic expression are closed off, the stakes become higher and the detonation, when it comes, will be quite spectacular. There are also some very nasty politicians around who are looking for ways to exploit hard economic times to turn South Africans against each other.

We live in an environment primed for change. The reason this book started with the Tunisian story is to make the point about how unexpectedly and how quickly the world can change, and how far that change can extend. The story of what started that December day in Sidi Bouzid shows how quickly we may find ourselves in a country entirely different from the one we inhabit today. Delivering his 'Rubicon' speech in August 1985, P.W. Botha made it clear that he rejected reform – but a decade later many of his former colleagues were joining the ANC. White business leaders, including those who had propped up the apartheid system, changed sides almost effortlessly. If you had suggested at the height of the struggle for democracy that liberation movement and trade union leaders, such as Cyril Ramaphosa and Trevor Manuel, would become mine owners and banking executives – the very capitalist crusaders they once fought – I wonder if even they would have seen it coming.

The transition that happened in South Africa in the 1990s was not a one-off event. It was the third in a series of South African transitions that have played themselves out in a now predictable cyclical pattern since the end of the Anglo-Boer War. The first happened in the decade between the end of that war and May 1910 when the Union of South Africa became a reality. The second came with the rise of apartheid after the defeat of General Smuts in the election of 1948. The third was the democratic transition of 1994. On each occasion the pattern was the same. A period of very weak economic performance and slowing increases (even declines) in living standards triggered a political realignment. Each realignment was in turn followed by relatively buoyant economic growth that secured a measure of political stability. The 1920s and 1930s were a very high growth era. High levels of economic growth were again experienced in the 1950s, 1960s and early 1970s. The late 1990s to mid-2000s saw good economic numbers. However, on each occasion when those growth trajectories turned downwards for the better part of a decade, this triggered the next transition. If the cyclical theory is correct, then we now stand on the verge of the fourth transition to a new political and economic status quo.

Don't think that a fourth transition has to mean a change for the worse – in fact, two of the scenarios developed in this book describe a South Africa that is much richer and more stable than the country today. Change, when it comes, is often for the better, even where the short-term trends leading up to the point of change have been negative. If you had told American civil rights movement leaders in the 1960s that within their own lifetimes there would be a black president in the White House, they might not have believed it. Just four decades ago China was a poor country of rural peasants led by a dogmatic Communist regime with limited global political influence. Today it is one of the engines of global economic growth, its military can project power around the world, it is (arguably) the global centre of anarcho-capitalism, its leaders lecture Western politicians about the dangers of protectionist trade policies, and forecasts suggest that over the next three decades its middle class may grow to exceed the population of the United States.

There will seldom be any clear warning long before the fact of the timing and direction of these transitions. Advance warning can best be obtained by reading the embryonic trends and extrapolating from these how things are likely to play out. Many people will resist the suggestion of profound imminent change based on embryonic trends alone and will demand harder evidence. But the evidence they seek is only going to appear during the process of change itself, by which stage it is too late to position oneself and respond to it. A common mistake is to underestimate the pace and extent of change and to plan instead for a number of slight permutations to the status quo – only to be caught off guard by real change when it happens. Very few companies or individuals are well positioned to anticipate and take advantage of change, and hence they experience a high degree of inertia that has its origins in a fear of the unknown and a craving for certainty. Sometimes it is too difficult to accept predictions of change because the future world being described is just too different from the one we inhabit today.

Even foreign powers with significant interests in the Middle East had little advance warning of just how unstable that region was about to become. Israeli analysts, who are very good at this sort of thing, did not anticipate the timing and complete extent of what they referred to from early on, quite incisively as things turned out, as the Arab Winter. Sometimes the bigger the organisation the more difficult it is to get it to accept the certainty of change.

But from the examples of the Arab Spring, to the American civil rights movement, China and our own history, massive change does happen, often against the grain of history and in conflict with once-dominant trends. Sometimes the change is for the better and other times it is for the worse. But when it comes it happens very rapidly and moves the society in which it happens into a totally different paradigm. The lesson is to be deeply sceptical about the longevity of the status quo, or about the belief that short-term trends are indicative of long-term futures. To be well positioned in a future South Africa, understand that change will occur *faster*, have *deeper* implications, and move the environment in which you live *further* than most analysts presently believe could possibly be the case.

The knowledge that a profound degree of political and economic change is on the way does not need to be intimidating or paralyse us with uncertainty. If we are willing to accept the inevitability of profound change, there are methodologies by means of which it is possible to develop a degree of certainty about what will happen tomorrow, and the day after, and the day after that, and to push that horizon out well beyond the next decade. These are tested methodologies that work, and in this book we will apply them so as to move past all the fear and uncertainty and understand what is going to happen between now and 2030.

If you read the first book in this series (*A Time Traveller's Guide to Our Next Ten Years*), published in 2014, you will already have some idea of how the process of getting to grips with the future works. In that book we set out four possible futures for South Africa for the morning after the 2024 election. In the first of these, the Wide Road, we suggested that, despite the odds, the ANC would stage an internal reformation and win massive popular support as the party turned the South African economy around. In the second scenario, the Narrow Road, we suggested that to survive politically, the ANC would be forced into a series of unpopular pro-capitalist reforms in a desperate bid to stage an economic recovery and would force those reforms onto the country against the wishes of a rebellious and hostile public. In the third scenario, the ANC would reject the need for economic reform and rather turn to destroying South Africa's democracy in a bid to cling to power. The fourth scenario suggested that the ANC would fail to introduce economic reforms and also fail in destroying democratic institutions, meaning that it would lose the election of 2024 and take South Africa into a new era of coalition politics.

Those scenarios were initially drawn with a stick in the sand during a long walk with South Africa's top scenario developer, Clem Sunter, along a Cape Town beach. He might not remember, but I asked him which scenario would materialise, and his answer was that one of them would happen a lot sooner than I expected. At that time the ANC governed every major metropolitan municipality other than Cape Town. Just over two years later the ANC had lost political control of almost all the Gauteng metros to the Democratic Alliance (DA), which meant the opposition was in some respects governing over more than 50% of South Africa's GDP, and South Africa was well on its way to a new era of coalition politics.

In the first book we stopped at the point of the scenarios and did not venture a view of which one would materialise. There were good, sound reasons for that decision – most importantly, that complex systems theory (explained in chapter 2) shows that small changes in the present conditions of a system will trigger massive shifts in its future, a concept popularised as the 'butterfly effect'. In retrospect, however, it proved to be a mistake not to make a call on which scenario would materialise, since almost every audience we have addressed over the past three years has asked us to single out which scenario we believe it will be. On most occasions this was the first question asked. This happened with such regularity that it prompted some amateur research into people and their craving for certainty. The results, which are briefly discussed in the introduction to chapter 2, were compelling enough to warrant that in this book we will go further, and despite the considerable risks, say which scenario it will be and what life will be like under that scenario. This will include answering tough questions, such as whether that scenario will offer us a prosperous future. Will South Africa be successful and peaceful? Will people get on with each other, and will black and white South Africans pull off the remarkable reconciliation that happened between English-speaking whites and the Afrikaners in the decades after the Anglo-Boer War? Or will it all just go wrong and, if so, how wrong? If it does 'go wrong', does that mean that we will simply remain poor and unequal – much as we are today? Or is that a naïve expectation, and will the creeping sense of foreboding that so many people now feel about the country be a precursor of something worse than any of us dares to imagine?

In getting to those answers, we are going to follow a series of steps. The first (in chapter 2) will be to look at how and why the world changes. That is important because it explains why scenario planning works and also explains the theory behind why a seemingly random act – such as that of Mohamed Bouazizi in a place as otherwise insignificant as Sidi Bouzid – can in fact change the world. If you don't understand the reasons for change and the theoretical underpinnings of scenario planning, then it is very difficult to believe that some of the conclusions that will be reached in this book could possibly play themselves out in a future South Africa.

Then in chapters 3, 4, 5 and 6 we take a deep dive into the socio-economic circumstances that South Africans live in, the standing of the economy, the true state of race relations, and how political trends are evolving. We will be looking for indicators of direction or pieces of information that may give us a good sense of where our country is headed. With that information in hand we will (in chapter 7) set out to craft a fresh set of scenarios for South Africa, each of which will describe a plausible future we may encounter – one year after the 2029 national elections.

Each of chapters 8, 9, 10 and 11 will take one of those scenarios and describe it in a great degree of detail. Those descriptions will be narratives written about the future. Think of them as reports, written in 2030, looking back at what has changed in South Africa and why it changed. Through all of this, piece by piece, and page by page, what will happen in our country in the period between now and 2030 will become apparent.

Chapter 2: Seeing very far ahead

Humans do not like uncertainty, and medical researchers have discovered the reasons why. In his book *On Intelligence*, Jeff Hawkins (inventor of the PalmPilot) writes, 'Your brain receives patterns from the outside world, stores them as memories, and makes predictions by combining what it has seen before and what is happening now. Prediction is not just one of the things your brain does. It is the primary function of the neo-cortex, and the foundation of intelligence.'

Psychologists say the craving for certainty is similar to cravings for oxygen or certain foods. Cigarette addiction would be a good example of such a craving. Humans are programmed to seek out certainty and then make decisions that are based on confidently knowing what will happen next. Denying the brain confidence in such certainty produces a physical response of great discomfort and even agitation – equivalent to what may happen if you deny cigarettes to a smoker. This is why the last nail-biting minutes of a very close rugby or cricket match produce such extremes of emotional behaviour – oscillations from elation to tears of despair and back again. During a briefing a client made the point that this is why train stations put up electric boards telling passengers in how many minutes the next train will arrive. It calms people on the platform and cuts down on aggressive and anti-social behaviour.

All of this presents a problem for economic and political analysts. If you think the anxiety around a rugby match is bad, try telling a retailer that it is unclear what consumer trends will do over the next quarter, or tell a room full of investors that currency trends have become difficult to predict. I have seen some corporate boards and strategists become quite emotional that there are scenarios that are at odds with their strategic plans. This is not that they disagreed with the scenario or challenged it on the basis of the facts or quality of argument – their response was neurologically driven, a natural human reaction triggered by the fear that comes with not knowing. It is a deeply troubling and uncomfortable sensation.

The sensation is made so much more extreme when life-changing decisions need to be taken. Parents want to know that they are taking the best long-term decisions for their children. Farmers want to know that the money they borrow to develop their farms or plant a crop will produce a return. Investors want to know that their assets are safe from expropriation by politicians. Politicians want to know that they will not lose their seats (and salaries) in future elections.

Just like smokers who succumb to the craving for a cigarette, when people succumb to the craving to know what lies in wait over the horizon they start forecasting. This can be very dangerous, as a forecaster is doing something quite extraordinary – he or she is saying that *one* particular set of circumstances will coincide with a particular point in future space and time. In two articles published in the *Harvard Business Review* in the 1980s, the forefather of modern scenario planning, the Frenchman Pierre Wack, explained that forecasting is highly dangerous because forecasts are often right. However, Wack wrote that they are only right because the world they were based on has not yet changed. When that world does change, precisely at the moment when the forecast would have been most useful, it is useless, and the forecaster has to go back to the drawing board and start the process again, inevitably setting himself or herself up for more failures. Wack worked for the oil company Shell, where he shot to global prominence when he accurately anticipated the oil price spike of the early 1970s, which caught the rest of the global oil industry largely off guard. He also has a tie to South Africa in that he helped to train the scenario planning team at Anglo American, which similarly shot to fame under Clem Sunter in the 1980s with the *High Road–Low Road* scenarios.

There is now a body of theoretical research that proves that the futures of countries and economies can never be accurately forecast.

This is the theory of systems, in particular an offshoot of that theory called complex systems theory. It is all very straightforward and easy to understand. Complex systems theory states that a typical complex system will display four characteristics:

Firstly, it is made up of a great many participants or actors that exist within the system. An ant colony would qualify. Weather and traffic patterns are complex systems. It is easy to see how South Africa (or any country), with tens of millions of people, tens of thousands of businesses, all manner of interest groups and a host of other actors, would qualify on this characteristic.

Secondly, these participants interact with each other within the system in pursuit of their goals. Ants do this. Climatological forces do, and so do cars and drivers in the morning traffic. In the case of an economy, the competition between businesses for customers is an example of such interaction. So too the efforts of competing activists or political parties. Every individual's pursuit of wealth and happiness is an example of such interaction.

These participants direct what is called 'feedback' into the system – this is its third characteristic. Participants that are satisfied with their progress in the system direct a type of feedback that seeks to maintain the status quo of the system. Participants that are unhappy direct a different type of feedback, which seeks to change the system. It is easy to identify this behaviour within a country. When university students went on the rampage at South African universities in 2015 and 2016, stormed the Union Buildings, and broke through the gates of the parliamentary precinct, that was an example of feedback that sought to change South Africa's status quo. Efforts to bring interdicts against the students and the deployment of the police on campuses were examples of attempts to maintain the status quo. In any system (or country), change happens when those actors seeking to change the system introduce a degree of feedback that overwhelms those that seek to maintain the status quo.

Finally, a complex system has a fourth attribute in respect of the interaction between its various participants; this is what is called an *emergent* characteristic. What this means is that the result of that interaction will be greater than the sum of its parts. Take the example of these simple equations below.

Imagine that there are five participants in a system (we will call it system X). If a participant is happy with the status quo of that system, he or she will contribute a nominal value of 2 to the system. If they are unhappy they contribute a 1.

In that case, where every actor in the system was happy, the system would look as follows:

System X is 2+2+2+2+2=10

Now let us imagine that one of the actors becomes unhappy and contributes a 1 to the system. In that case, the system would look as follows:

System X is 2+2+2+2+1=9

The system has changed from a ten to a nine – a significant change but not a dramatic or earth-shattering one.

Let us now imagine that system X is a complex system that multiplies, instead of adding together, the feedback exerted by its participants. Where all the participants were happy the system would look as follows:

System X is 2x2x2x2x2=32

Now see what happens when one actor becomes disillusioned with the system and seeks to change the status quo:

System X is 2x2x2x2x1=16

The system has changed from a value of 32 to a 16 – a dramatic change.

A good example of the emergent property of complex systems in action is the traffic. Many of us have to struggle through the traffic every morning.

Thousands of other motorists struggle with us as we all compete to get to our destinations. If we all co-operate, the traffic might flow predictably if slowly. However, if just one driver breaks out of the status quo and causes an accident, she or he can trigger gridlock, which delays thousands of other motorists. They in turn delay many more thousands of other people who are waiting for them in meetings and places of business. Deals can be lost, money can be made and lost – all because of the act of just one participant in a system of thousands of others, and there is nothing that the thousands can do to change that.

It is that emergent property of complex systems that makes any attempt at long-term forecasting in a complex or volatile environment very difficult. You might as well try to forecast traffic patterns for your commute tomorrow morning. To do that, you would need to anticipate and account for the future actions of every other driver on the road. It cannot be done and, therefore, even if your forecast is 'right', this would only be because the world you are forecasting has not yet changed.

Now the Arab Spring can be better understood as a consequence of the emergent property of complex systems, as this explains how Mohamed Bouazizi in Sidi Bouzid was able to set in motion events that had such an extraordinary effect on the world. His example highlights perfectly the futility of trying to forecast, to a single point in space and time, the long-term future of any economy, country or region of the world.

We are faced therefore with a conundrum. On the one hand we have to account for the human craving for certainty about the future. On the other hand we have to work within the constraints imposed by the emergent property of complex systems. The solution lies in scenario planning.

Many clients are surprised to hear that scenario planning is not forecasting. The two methods are quite distinct. Whereas the forecaster seeks to define precisely a single future point in space and time, the scenario planner is seeking to identify a number of equally plausible points in future space and time. The distinction is that to the forecaster the future is a singular concept – there can be only one future and his or her job is to identify it. For the scenario planner, the future is a plural concept.

There will always be more than one plausible future, and each of these must be respected as having a roughly equal degree of plausibility. It is only by accepting this that it becomes possible to overcome the crippling effects of the emergent property of complex systems.

At this point more than one client has suggested that it all sounds a bit hopeless. What is the point of identifying a series of roughly equally plausible futures? How can a decision be taken? What should she or he tell the shareholders and the board? That client has just run into reality and is now in danger of succumbing to the temptation to start forecasting.

Fortunately there is an acceptable compromise.

Our first answer to such a client will be that scenario planning projects are not going to throw up hundreds of different futures. Most scenario projects will deliver between two and four different future worlds. Our second answer will be for the client to develop a strategy for each world and then adopt the one that seems to align most closely with the current environment. Not for a moment, however, should that strategic decision be taken at the cost of jettisoning the other scenarios. The client should develop a series of indicators indicative of the emergence of each of the other scenarios and be prepared to turn on a dime the moment it seems that a new scenario has become most probable.

Take a practical example. Many clients ask advice on how ANC economic policy will change. A forecaster could provide an answer, and the client might use that answer to build a strategy for his operations in South Africa. A scenario planner would provide two or three different sets of answers, probably going as far as compelling the client to face up to the question of what economic policy would look like if the ANC were no longer around. A decision could then be made about which of the answers the current climate seems to suggest as the most probable, and the strategy that applies to that scenario can be put into operation. But when the climate changes – and it will – the client already knows exactly what to do, while competitors are scrambling to figure out what just happened and how to respond.

Does the singling out of one scenario not contradict the complex systems basis of scenario planning? To an extent it does, but reality leaves no alternative and as long as it is not done, with the result of writing off the other scenarios, it offers the best solution to the conundrum that exists between the prescripts of complexity theory and emergence, on the one hand, and the neurological craving to know what will happen tomorrow, on the other.

The differences between forecasts and scenarios are therefore the following:

Forecasts develop a single certain future around which a strategy must be built. There is not much early warning that the forecast may be wrong. There is no fall-back position or Plan B if it is wrong. New strategy must be developed in the midst of the chaos of change.

Scenarios usually develop two to four varied futures. A strategy is built around each future, and indicators are available to show which future is most likely to materialise. If the markers change it is easy to change strategy. In a well-built set of scenarios nothing should be able to occur that takes the company, country or government that commissioned the scenarios by surprise. They have a contingency plan for each eventuality. Somewhat counterintuitively, by agreeing to work within the constraints imposed by the emergent property of complex systems, the client who has agreed to accept the plural nature of the future actually has far more certainty about the future than the client who chooses to rely on a single forecast.

How do you create a set of scenarios? The methodology most commonly employed is tried and tested and has been used with variations by consultancies around the world for over 30 years.

The first step is to identify what the client actually wants to know, and over what time frame he or she wants to know it. In other words, what is the focal question and over what time horizon must the question be answered? The question can be very broad or extremely narrow. One request may be to know how banks might be exposed to land reform policy over the next three to four years. Another may be what the long-term (ten- to twenty-year) implications of current mining policy might be for greenfield mining exploration in South Africa. An activist group may want to know what the worst-case outcome for civil rights might be in order to test the likely efficacy of a contingency plan it had developed. A media company may want to know what the effect of 'view on demand' technology might be for traditional radio and television stations. In the case of this book we want to know what life will be like in the South Africa of 2030.

The second step is to identify every economic, social and political force that might have an impact on that decision. The net must be cast very wide, and several hundred indicators or pieces of information may be gathered. In the case of this book, four chapters will be devoted to explaining current economic, social and political trends.

The third step is to gather those trends into a series of groups or families of related major trends. Ideally we want to get down to 40 or 50 major trends, each of which will have a definitive influence on the question the scenarios seek to address.

The fourth step is to rank those trends according to the impact they are likely to have on the core question that the scenarios are trying to answer, and the uncertainty associated with that impact. This is done on a graph with two axes such as the one set out on page 35. The left axis measures relative uncertainty and the bottom axis measures relative impact. Trends that are grouped towards the lower left corner of the graphic will have a relatively limited impact on the scenarios, and there is relatively little uncertainty about what that impact will be. Trends grouped towards the top right corner will have a relatively high degree of impact on the question the scenarios are trying to answer, and there is great uncertainty about what that impact will be. It is these types of trends against which business and political strategists need to test their contingency plans if they are to be confident that those contingencies can anticipate and respond effectively to sudden and dramatic shifts in the environments they operate in.

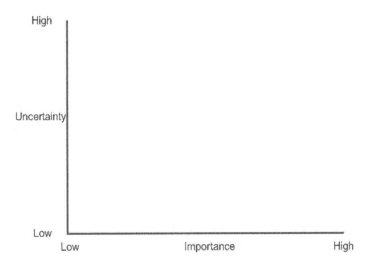

The fifth step is to determine what those sudden shifts are likely to be. This is done by taking the trend of greatest impact and plotting it against that of greatest uncertainty on a matrix such as that set out on page 36. The matrix in turn delivers four quadrants, and each of these will become one scenario. The robustness of this methodology is that it takes the greatest uncertainties faced by an organisation and multiplies these by the trends that will have the greatest impact on that organisation. To demonstrate how this works, the matrix provides an example of a set of mining and natural gas scenarios. That hypothetical study suggested that geological conditions would have the greatest impact on the future of the mining industry in South Africa, while mining policy was the greatest uncertainty faced by the industry. The matrix suggested that the likely best-case scenario for mining was Scenario 1 in which generous geological conditions coexisted with enabling mining policy. The worst case was Scenario 3 in which increasingly difficult geological conditions (very deep gold seams and limited natural gas reserves, for example) coexisted with a hostile mining investment climate.

With the matrix plotted, we now have direction. We know that the future will fall within one of the four quadrants of the matrix. But we do not yet know which one, nor do we know with precision what each of the four futures will be like. The latter problem is solved by going

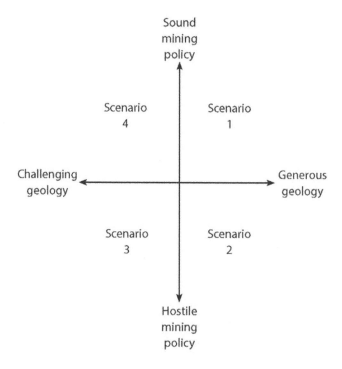

back to the original research conducted in step two and setting out how each of the trends identified in our original scan of the broader economic and policy environment would be likely to evolve in each scenario. In other words, we have to write a story of what life is like in that future. In a sense it is a fictional story because it has not yet happened. But the story will occupy a strange no-man's-land between fiction and reality as it will be based on hard data and trends that we know are real and from which we can easily extrapolate. The aim here is to provide the sense of suspended disbelief that we are already in that future. That is very important because the emotions evoked must inspire the readers of the scenarios to act in the present to realise the best outcomes and avoid the worst. They must recoil in horror from the worst outcomes and work very hard at achieving the best. In this sense, good scenario sets often turn out to be self-fulfilling prophecies in that they inspire management teams, corporations or even countries to reach the best-case scenarios.

The final step is to identify a number of markers or indicators indicative of the likelihood of the current and most probable scenario changing to another. By tracking those indicators closely, there will be adequate advance warning of which scenario is going to happen.

At a recent investment seminar I set out four plausible outcomes for South Africa in 2024 and what their implications were for people with considerable savings and investments. A member of the audience, somewhat agitated, rose to enquire why I could not tell him which of the four would happen. I did tell him, but also recited all the warnings about the emergent property of complex systems and that, rather than obsessing over which scenario would materialise, investors might be better off accepting inherent uncertainty, developing an investment strategy for each scenario, and reading the environment very closely to shift strategy as circumstances in the country changed. Very few companies and organisations do that well, but it is essentially what sets strong strategic planning teams apart from weak ones and robust companies from less successful ones – especially those invested in volatile emerging markets.

Many of the companies we have worked with have found that developing a strategy for four scenarios is not actually much more demanding than developing a strategy for one. They can then confidently adopt the strategy that aligns most closely with the scenario they deem most probable. But they are securely positioned to switch strategy at a moment's notice if there are sudden policy or market changes and another scenario becomes more probable. Compare their position with that of a company that rather chooses to rely on the single forecast of a consultant who has the confidence to say that he knows how the future will evolve. When markets shift and policies change, that company may find itself in a crisis. The forecast they choose to rely on has no value. They have to go back to the drawing board, do new research, and develop new strategies for the changed environment. However, the company that planned through scenarios will be many months, even years, ahead of them. The same applies to families planning for their futures in South Africa.

In this book we are going to follow the methodology given here. The outcome will be a set of precise descriptions of what life in our country will be like in 2030. Each will be accompanied by five easily identifiable indicators of which scenario it will be. The result will be to provide more than a decade of advance warning of where we are all headed – more than enough time to make a plan to capitalise on the best that South Africa will offer and hedge against the worst. There will be no excuse to say we did not see it coming.

Chapter 3: A good story to tell about a better life for all

In a speech to Parliament in 2016, the Minister of Human Settlements, Lindiwe Sisulu, quoted an IRR report to the effect that 'service delivery in South Africa should on balance be seen as a success'. She also quoted the economist Mike Schüssler as describing service delivery as a 'great success'. Lies and a cynical misrepresentation of our research and Mike Schüssler's views? Not at all. The ANC in the provinces that it governs and the DA in the Western Cape have in fact done a great deal more to improve the living standards of people (rich and poor) than many analysts are willing to admit and many South Africans understand.

The data tells the story.

Start with electricity – a key ingredient for living a better life. The graphic overleaf tracks the change in delivery of electricity to families across the nine provinces between 1996 and 2015. Take the Eastern Cape as an example – the poorest and arguably worst governed of South Africa's nine provinces. The graphic shows that in 1996 approximately 70% of families in that province *did not* have electricity, but by 2016 that percentage had come down to 15% – a remarkable reversal. The same is true across all the provinces and therefore for South Africa as a whole.

Similar successes have been achieved in the delivery of clean water. The next graphic sets out the delivery of clean piped water to families over the past two decades. It shows that in 1996 just 7.2 million households in South Africa had a clean water source, but this figure had increased to 14.3 million by 2016. This represents almost a doubling of the number of households with access to a clean water source.

Very few societies could match the pace of South Africa's electricity and water delivery successes of the past twenty years. That this surprises many South Africans shows just how skewed the story of our first twenty

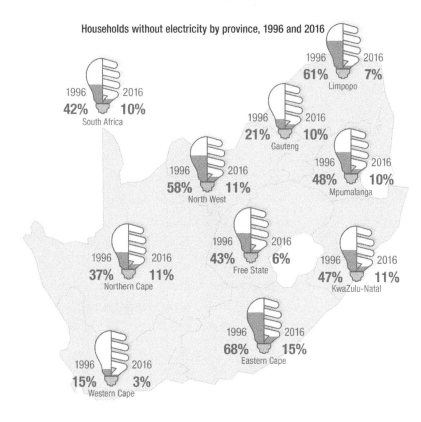

Households without electricity by province, 1996 and 2016

Households with access to piped water, 1996 and 2016

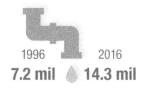

1996   2016

7.2 mil 💧 **14.3 mil**

years as a democracy has become. In many respects we became a country that celebrated the bad news and rejected the good. When the IRR launched a campaign highlighting South Africa's actual socio-economic progress (approximately five years ago), we faced extraordinary criticism. One newspaper editor penned an editorial that we should not try to ingratiate ourselves with ruling party politicians. I received concerned messages from far afield asking if something had gone wrong with the

IRR. Most revealing was the shock with which government leaders and ANC politicians received the news. They seem genuinely surprised to hear that they had done something right. A group of ANC leaders nodded in sombre agreement during a meeting in 2015 when we explained how one of their main successes – service delivery – was being used as a weapon to 'beat you [them] with in the media'.

The story of South Africa's success in increasing living standards is not restricted to water and electricity. It extends across the breadth of indicators that would commonly be used to benchmark living standards.

Housing is a good example. The following graphic sets out the proportion of households in 1996 and again in 2015 based on the type of housing they occupy. The graphic shows, for example, that in 1996 64% of South Africans had access to formal housing. By 2015 that proportion had increased to 78%. Over the same period, the proportion of South Africans accommodated in informal housing had declined from 16% to 14%.

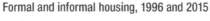

Formal and informal housing, 1996 and 2015

1996	2015	1996	2015
64%	78.1%	16%	14.1%

Formal housing   Informal housing

The proportions are somewhat modest, but that is because of the rapid growth in the number of households in the country. Consider that the number of families living in a formal house has increased from under 6 million in 1996 to over 12 million today, and the data appears much more impressive. Over the same period the number of households living in shacks also increased from 1.45 million to 2.28 million. But the extraordinary thing is that for every shack newly erected after 1996, around ten formal houses were built. The impression generated in the popular media that we are a country being overwhelmed by poverty and desperation, and that little has changed for the good since our democratic transition, is simply not true.

Living standards were further bolstered by the rollout of what is the most expansive social welfare system of any emerging market. The graph below shows that in 1994 there were approximately 2 million South Africans receiving monthly cash grants from the state. Starting around 2001, that number began to escalate and by 2015 there were more than 16 million grant recipients – almost a third of the population.

Number of social grant beneficiaries, 1994–2016

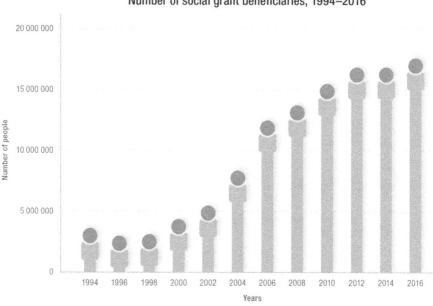

Many conservative analysts would be critical of the paragraphs above – that welfare and state-led service delivery should be seen as one of our successes as a society. Their argument is that the extent of welfare roll-out is an indictment of our country, as it reflects the inability of the economy to place people in a position to work and improve their own standard of living. They are, of course, correct, and welfare cannot be a substitute for earned income.

There are also devastating statistics that run parallel to those relating to the social grants rollout. These measure what we call the dependency ratio or the number of people employed compared with the number of people with grants. In 2001 that ratio was 310 to 100. In other words, there were 310 people with jobs for every 100 people receiving grants.

By 2014, however, things had become horribly skewed and there were 90 people with jobs for every 100 people with grants. Rather than becoming a source of income support, social grants had become an alternative to earned income.

That we have developed a system of welfare dependency is nothing to be proud of. However, the point that must also be made, and is too often overlooked, is that South Africa's welfare and service delivery programmes have had the effect of raising the basic living standards of many very poor people. For example, the proportion of children under the age of five who are malnourished has fallen from roughly 15%, when the grants rollout first picked up momentum, to under 5% today. Overall, South Africans are materially better off because of those programmes, and so is the consumer economy as a whole.

So important did this grant income become to overall economic activity that a number of retail and financial services groups in South Africa privately concede that much of their growth of the past twenty years could not have happened in the absence of the welfare programme. It must be a bitter irony for the champions of state-driven social welfare economics that their greatest champions include large multinational retail corporations, while the grants have done relatively little to provide a sustainable way out of poverty for the poor.

The grants can also be viewed as a double-edged sword. In the short term they work to the political advantage of the government of the day, but in the longer term they are liable to become a problem. This happens when, as now, it is no longer possible to increase the grants by the rate of inflation – considering especially that the rate of inflation experienced by poor households is very much higher than that experienced by richer ones, as the poor spend more of their income on high-inflation items such as fuel, transport and food.

We have tracked the increases in old-age pension grant values over time and there is a predictable pattern. Between 2000 and 2002 grant values were increased by approximately 6% per annum. But in 2003, before the 2004 national election, the increase was 12.8%. Between 2005 and 2007 those same grants increased in value by under 6% per annum. But in 2008 and 2009 they increased by an average of over 7%, despite the global financial crisis. In the 2014 election year they increased by 7.1%, which is roughly a 40% higher increase than the increases of just over 5% in the immediately preceding years – and this despite the very tough fiscal conditions facing the government. The government understands very well that to let the real (inflation-adjusted) value of grants slip will trigger a political reaction it cannot easily survive. The intensity of the backlash is likely to be inversely proportional to the political support that the grants initially helped to secure for the government.

The combined effects of successful service delivery and growing social welfare rollout can be measured with LSM or Living Standards Measure data. LSM data groups people into categories numbered from 1 to 10, based on their living standards. The categories are determined by the things people have access to, such as vacuum cleaners or satellite television. In 2001, less than a decade into the democratic era, approximately 40% of South Africans fell into the lowest three living standard categories. However, by 2015 that percentage had fallen to just over 10%. There had been a remarkable outflow of people from the lower LSM categories into the higher categories. The changes in LSM data reflect changes that we see in incomes and expenditure data; the most important is that the real disposable per capita income of households has increased by 44% since 1994.

It follows that as living standards and incomes have increased, the middle class must have grown. In 2015 the IRR published a study that estimated that the size of the black middle class was beginning to approximate that of the white middle class. Data showed that more suburban home sales were taking place to black people than to white people. The combined total buying power of black people had long overtaken that of whites. Data from the Commission for Employment Equity shows that the proportion of top and senior managers in the economy who happen to be black has doubled since 2000. National and provincial government and state-owned enterprises show near-perfect demographic representation in their senior workforces. A survey of 800 private companies suggested that in 2015 approximately 4 in every 10 senior managers were black, as were 5 in every 10 junior managers – another remarkable reversal if we consider the country of twenty years before.

A major impetus behind the growth of the middle class has been the transformation of the civil service. There are just over 2 million civil servants in the country. Some of them might not have been particularly productive, but the civil service did play a very important role in being the incubator of a future black middle class. The children of civil servants are likely to have received better education and grown up in more prosperous circumstances than their parents. They are well positioned, as the second generation of the black middle class, to break into the private sector. Their position has further been supported by the fact that average wage settlements (or increases) in South Africa have tended to be 2 percentage points higher than inflation over the past twenty years. Much of this can be accounted for by the advocacy efforts of public sector unions.

Another useful indicator of the growth of the middle class relates to aircraft take-offs and landings in South Africa. These have increased by 25% over the past decade, some of which is accounted for by tourists – but the balance is a number that supports the thesis of a growing domestic middle class. The story of the rising middle class can also be told through the motor-vehicle industry in South Africa. The graph on page 46 shows the number of new vehicle sales in South Africa over the past twenty years. In 1995 altogether 255,817 new cars were sold. In 2016 that number had almost doubled to 485,000. We know that the white population has not grown over the past two decades, so much of the increase in vehicle sales must be attributed to black buyers. This aligns with our estimate that the overall middle class has doubled in size since 1994.

Despite improvements in living standards, and the growing middle class, South Africa remains an unequal society when viewed in terms

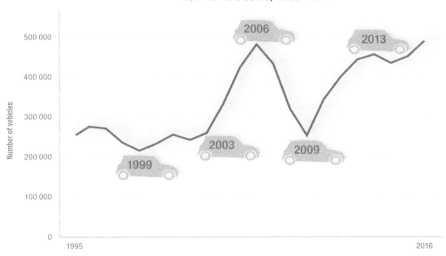

New vehicle sales, 1995–2016

of income levels. Data shows that just over 15% of households (or families) in South Africa spend more than R10,000 per month. A great effort is made in the media and by politicians to display this as a racial schism. But that neat 'black is poor, white is rich' split no longer applies to South Africa. There are now 1.4 million black families spending more than R10,000 per month as opposed to under 1 million white families. Just on 40% of white families actually spend less than that amount. Whites are on balance not very wealthy. Many white middle-class families, like many black middle-class families, live pay-check to pay-check, just getting by with paying the bond, school fees, credit card debt and car repayments that are the month-to-month challenges of maintaining a middle-class lifestyle in South Africa. Household debt-to-savings levels are much higher than they were in 1994, suggesting that what is often seen as household wealth is simply the effect of credit extension. Real investable wealth is the preserve of very few people.

In any event, too much is made of inequality as a problem in our society. The increase in the Gini coefficient (a measure of inequality) that South Africa has experienced relates mainly to the rise of the black middle class and is an expected transitionary phenomenon in any society that graduates from being very poor to being better off. As more of the society achieves middle-class status over the next twenty or thirty years, inequality levels will moderate.

This is of great importance – to grow the middle class and education is the primary predictor of whether or not a child born in South Africa will attain a middle-class standard of living. Overall education levels have improved over the past two decades. In 1995, 19% of people aged twenty and older had a matric pass as their highest level of education and 2.9% had a degree. However, by 2015 those percentages had increased to 28% and 5% respectively – numbers that must be weighed against persistent criticism of declining standards. In line with the growing middle class, black enrolment in the lower grades of some private schools is beginning to exceed that of whites. The much longer-term trends look even better. The graph below tells the story of the narrowly defined black matric class since 1955.

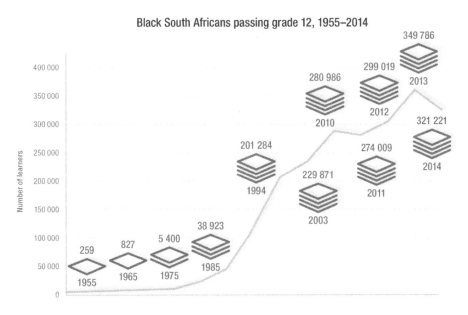

Black South Africans passing grade 12, 1955–2014

The graph shows that in 1955 there were 259 black children who passed their matric exams. Not much changed in the 1960s and 1970s, but in the 1980s and 1990s the number of black children writing and passing matric escalated significantly to reach over 300,000 today.

Improvements in school education have in turn made possible some quite extraordinary increases in the number of people getting into, and graduating from, university. The graphic below shows the increase in the number of people enrolled at university in South Africa. In 1995 the number was 575,412, but almost twenty years later, in 2014, it had increased to 969,154, or by over 60%. Much of the increase is accounted for by black students, many of whom were the first in their families to obtain a tertiary education. In 1991, for example, there were 44 white students who graduated with degrees in engineering from a university for every 1 black graduate. By 2014, the number of black engineering graduates exceeded the number of whites by a ratio of 1.7 to 1.

University enrolments, 1995 and 2014

1995
575 412

2014
969 154

The pattern of progress seen in the engineering graduate statistics is repeated across almost all fields of tertiary study. It is clearly inaccurate to suggest, as many activists and commentators do, that there has been no substantive transformation in higher education since 1994.

When we are asked for advice on making sense of South Africa's social and living standards statistics, we warn that certainty is an illusion and that seeking it in socio-economic data is dangerous. Very often within the same field (and even within the same data set) you will find at first glance contradictory trends. Evidence of socio-economic progress co-exists with evidence of terrible failures. The temptation is to conclude that the one view must be correct and the other wrong. More often than not, however, both are right. Critical to understanding socio-economic data is the ability to accept that there can be much truth in each of two seemingly opposing views. Analyses that overcome that complexity to reach the certainty implicit in conclusions of 'right' or 'wrong' are as a rule too simplistic. Being able to read the good with the bad, and understand the truth in both, is what sets the good analysts apart from the less proficient ones.

Education is a prime example, as, notwithstanding the good that has been achieved in overall improvements in education levels and the many successes of higher education, the majority of our schools perform badly. Three particular problems stand out.

The first is that the drop-out rate in the school system is very high. Of the approximately 1 million children who enrol in grade 1 every year, only half will progress to matric. This attrition essentially happens between grades 10 and 12 – the final years of the school system.

The second is that very few of the children who remain in school will pass the most important subjects, such as Mathematics and Science, with good grades. In fact, on current trends, of the approximately 1 million children who enrol in grade one, only 15,000–20,000 (or 1.5%–2%) can be expected to pass Mathematics in matric with a grade of 70% or higher. In 2013 only 11,965 pupils of what had been a grade 1 class of over a million pupils twelve years earlier passed Physical Science in matric with a grade of 70% or higher.

The graphic overleaf neatly sets out both problems. It shows the progression of the grade 10 class of 2012 through the school system. In that year (2012) in grade 10 there were 1,103,495 pupils. However, when that cohort reached matric in 2014 there were only 532,860 pupils left in the class. Of that reduced number, 403,874 passed matric, 150,752 obtained a bachelor's pass, and 120,523 passed maths. It must be kept in mind that we are reporting here on what the Department of Basic Education considers to be a pass – a grade of well below 50%.

The third problem in school education is that, despite sufficient financial resources, only 17% of schools in the country have a stocked library and only 18% have a laboratory. The challenges in education have little to do with financial resources, although activists choose to blame poor education outcomes in some schools on the fact that schools in richer areas have more money. But the government provides roughly equivalent grants to schools in poor and rich areas. Furthermore, both as a percentage of GDP and as a percentage of total government expenditure,

Throughput for the Grade 10 class of 2012

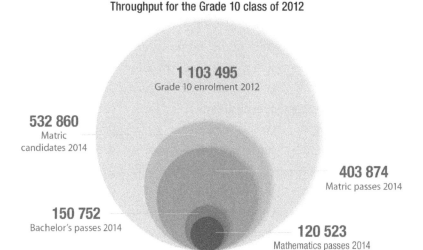

1 103 495
Grade 10 enrolment 2012

532 860
Matric
candidates 2014

403 874
Matric passes 2014

150 752
Bachelor's passes 2014

120 523
Mathematics passes 2014

South Africa does comparatively well in terms of school expenditure. For example, a World Bank report found that South Africa actually spends proportionally more on education in GDP terms than Spain, Poland, the Philippines, Chile, Uganda, Indonesia and India – among many other countries. Yet data from international studies shows that South Africa's education outcomes lag far behind those of most emerging markets.

The difference between top schools and schools that perform badly has a lot more to do with the management of the financial resources invested in that school than with the amount of money invested. Schools with strong management leadership and an involved parent body will produce better results than those held hostage by trade unions or run by bureaucrats. Improving the quality of schooling will therefore have less to do with money than with allowing parents and communities to take full control of schools in their communities.

Nor is there much convincing data to suggest that the tide at schools is turning. On the contrary, the number of children passing Mathematics with a grade of 70% or higher fell by 34% between 2008 and 2014. It follows that, despite the progress made in higher education, too few children will go on to get a good university qualification. Today just over 5% of South Africans over the age of 50 have a degree from a university (a figure that has nonetheless nearly doubled since 1994). Yet data from the labour market shows that for people without a tertiary qualification, less than half can expect to find work as compared with over 80% of those with a good degree. Match that with the fact that the government says it does not have the money to subsidise properly the education of deserving but poor university students, and there is little short-term hope that overall levels of educational achievement will increase. (As an aside, IRR analysts have shown that higher education could be properly subsidised within existing budget constraints through cutting the civil service – this has not happened, as the government is for the time being more afraid of civil servants than of students.) In fact, the danger exists that our universities may begin to perform a lot worse. The protests at campuses that gained so much media attention in late 2015 and again in 2016 have been skilfully exploited by politicians to erode the autonomy of those institutions. We also know from budget projections that the resources to finance those institutions properly will, in all probability, never be made available. The likelihood is that our public universities will become increasingly beholden to the state while losing the capacity to retain top skills and teaching programmes. Ironically, therefore, the radical push for transformation of campuses, driven by students and some academics, will in all likelihood disable the universities and halt, for a considerable time, the very positive trajectory they had experienced in the initial years after 1994.

Our critics ask why, if we are correct in suggesting that living standards have improved so quickly, there is so much violent protest action and anti-social behaviour in our society. Why, if things have gone well, do we have this feeling of impending revolution and that the stability of the country will not hold?

The answer is because of rising, and now unmet, expectations. As life improves in any society, people begin to expect continued improvement in their living standards. Where the economy becomes unable to secure such improvements, a dramatic political reaction is likely to be triggered – exactly as we see in South Africa today. Ironically, it is politically dangerous to raise living standards if you do not have the means to sustain the initial improvements that your welfare and development policies may bring about – and it is precisely this phenomenon that has caught up with the ANC. The danger becomes so much greater when your progress in improving living standards has been made possible mainly through the redistribution of wealth – since you are not placing people in a position where through employment and entrepreneurship they can take control of improving their own lives. There are few societies that could show levels of wealth redistribution similar to South Africa without triggering an economic collapse. Just think that if you are in the top individual income tax bracket you pay 40% of the income earned through your hard work to support the living standards, education, healthcare and security of other people. That is the equivalent of paying all the income you earn from January to late May every year to someone else – yet politicians and social justice activists suggest that the middle classes 'do nothing' to help the poor and build a better society. With South Africa's tax-to-GDP ratio reaching dangerous levels, there is very little room left to squeeze money out of South Africa's middle classes.

Do not allow our argument about the socio-economic progress South Africa has made to lull you into even the slightest sense of complacency about the future stability of our country. It is a terrible mistake to take the progress South Africa has made as an indication that things are good and that everything will work out for the best – that self-same progress feeds the growing frustrations.

The joint crises of rising expectations matched with high levels of dependency come together in the life experience of young South Africans – who now represent the first and most prominent of five socio-economic threats to our stability as a country. Research we have done into what is controversially referred to as the 'born-free' generation drew attention to what is called the NEET rate. NEET stands for people who are Not in Education, Employment or Training. To get a sense of the size of our powder keg, just think that South Africa's NEET rate for people in their twenties is around 50%. The extent and nature of many violent protests is in turn a reflection of the frustration that arises from the NEET rate. Corroboration for the frustration, if any were needed, comes in the form of polling data that shows young people are desperate for work.

Somewhat unusually, we rate healthcare trends, and especially policy trends, as the second greatest threat to social stability. Healthcare trends are dominated by the devastating effect of the irrational HIV and AIDS policies of the government of Thabo Mbeki in the early 2000s. The following graph shows that the antenatal HIV prevalence rate increased from 0.7% in 1990 to 30% in 2012. The pain and suffering inflicted on South African society as a consequence was without parallel.

HIV prevalence rate among women attending antenatal clinics, 1990–2012

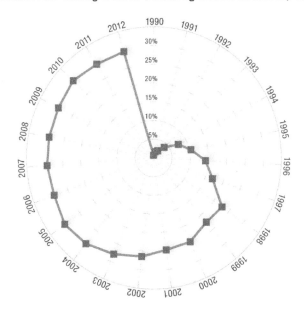

In the absence of proper care and treatment, people began to die at an alarming rate as the government advised poor people to treat HIV with a concoction of lemon juice and garlic. In 1997 there were 13,672 people aged 20 to 24 who died in the country. By 2013 that figure had almost doubled to 25,486. Life expectancy fell quickly. It reached 62 years in 1994 but bottomed out at 51 years in 2006. It took the defeat of

Thabo Mbeki and the incoming administration of Jacob Zuma to put in place a sensible treatment and prevention campaign.

In 2000, at the peak of the denialist policy, there were approximately 640,000 annual new HIV infections. By 2015 that number was down by more than half to 320,000. That is still almost 1,000 new infections per day, which means that, despite the better performance, South Africa's HIV/AIDS crisis is far from over – as many frustrated health activists will attest. Because of better care and awareness policies, life expectancy levels are again on the rise and, if current trends continue, they should reach 65 by 2020. However, even at these levels they remain far behind the levels in comparable emerging markets such as 77 in Mexico and 75 in China.

Incredibly, despite the burden that HIV and AIDS placed on the public healthcare system, progress was made on a number of benchmark health-care indicators, from diarrhoea incidence to immunisation rates. The graphic below shows that the proportion of children being immunised has increased from below 70% to 90% since 2001 – one of the best meas-ures of the efficacy of public healthcare programmes.

Immunisation rates, 2001–2014

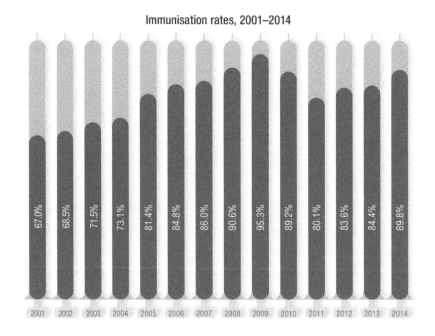

However, the burden that HIV and AIDS left in its wake consumed resources that should otherwise have been invested in improving the quality of public healthcare facilities. It also increased the disease burden on those facilities. Being short of resources (less than half of doctors work in the public sector), the state is desperate to redirect resources out of the private sector and into the public sector. The risk is that if their efforts go as far as harming the quality of the private healthcare sector, not to mention doing something unwise such as trying to nationalise health insurance funds, South Africa will struggle to retain its small, taxpaying middle class. No country that fails to offer world-class healthcare can retain a middle class. It will take just a few bad healthcare policy decisions over the next decade to trigger a mass middle-class exodus and economic activity and tax revenues will plummet.

The third threat to our social stability is very closely related to the second and takes the form of family structures. HIV and AIDS exacerbated probably the most damaging and evil aspect of the apartheid system – the breakdown of South African family life. Today there are roughly 19 million children living in South Africa. Yet only a third of these, roughly 6.5 million, live with both their parents. Roughly another third (about 7.5 million) live with one parent. The balance of just over 5 million live in households where they may seldom see their parents. South Africa is therefore a country with fractured family bonds. This is important because strong family bonds are the vehicle through which values are transferred in a society. When they do not exist, or are impaired, then transferring proper values from one generation to the next becomes difficult. This is not a criticism of single parents – many of whom do a heroic job and often a better job than many two-parent families – but research is unambiguous in showing that children raised without fathers, in particular, are more likely to engage in risky sexual behaviour or become involved in anti-social and even criminal behaviours.

For many years we had struggled to answer the question why South Africa has such extraordinary levels of violent crime, or why it became the centre of the global HIV pandemic, but we never really had a compelling answer. We had been a violent politically oppressed and poor society – but that was equally true for many other countries. The answer came to us about five years ago when we received a grant from the Anglo American Chairman's Fund to conduct research into families in South Africa. It was in the course of that work that we felt for the first time we knew the answer. It was family breakdown and therefore the inability of the society to imbue generations of young people with appropriate values. We estimated in the course of that work that a third of children would grow up in an environment where they never saw anyone go to work. The closest they saw was their relatives queuing for a grant from the government. There can be little doubt that much of the anti-social, violent and destructive behaviour we see from young people relates to weak family structures, and that our social fabric as a country will only ever be healed if we learn to build better and stronger family bonds.

Considering how important this is, it is frightening that family structures and values are not a higher policy priority in South Africa. By this is not meant the conservative idea of a man and a woman raising two children, but rather that a loving and supportive environment is necessary to shape responsible young people. Too few children in our country receive that support – and it shows in the anti-social and violent behaviour of many 'youths'.

Electricity shortages are the fourth threat to South Africa's stability. Our estimates suggest that current supply levels and anticipated new electricity infrastructure developments will be sufficient to support economic growth levels of roughly 2%. This is therefore the speed limit on economic growth. We do not, at this point, buy the story that Eskom has turned any corners. That the lights remained on in South Africa for much of 2015 and 2016 (after the serious blackouts and load-shedding of the immediately preceding years) was chiefly a result of the economy slumping, and therefore insufficient demand existed to exhaust supply. The real question to ask about electricity is whether there will be sufficient capacity to meet demand from economic growth rates of between

5% and 6%. Current supply levels are estimated to peak at just over 40,000 megawatts towards the end of this decade. A figure of closer to 50,000 will be necessary to support the economic growth levels required to secure a steep reduction in the unemployment rate. The risk is not just one of limited supply but also of the electrical grid destabilising and large areas of the country losing power, necessitating what some former Eskom insiders describe as a 'black-start', which is an effort to turn the power on again on a countrywide scale. There is some doubt about how quickly this could be done and whether Eskom has the in-house skills to do it. If we do lose power on a national scale that means no internet, no cell phones, limited banking and financial services, and general pandemonium.

The fifth threat to our social stability is water or, rather, the lack of it. Droughts exacerbated by the incompetent management of infrastructure could see large areas of the country lose water supplies. Research conducted into water policy shows that political and ideological interference in such policy, not climate and rainfall patterns, represents the greatest threat to South Africa's future water supply. Already many small towns have had to deal with the inconvenience of losing water supply or receiving only an intermittent supply, often for many months. These shortages are so serious that there are several cases of children having died from drinking toxic water. In one case we examined, the deaths resulted directly from the fact that the municipality did not appoint qualified people to run its water infrastructure. To some extent, smaller towns can deal with these crises through sinking boreholes and ferrying in water trucks. But what if larger centres lose water? Water interruptions in Grahamstown, for example, have previously forced Rhodes University to send its students home. In 2016 Kroonstad in the Free State essentially ran dry, and so did Aliwal North in the Eastern Cape.

Violent crime is a 'sixth factor' that should have been a destabilising influence but for the fact that we have adapted so well to living with its consequences. It is a war zone out there. Half a million people have been murdered in South Africa since 1994. This is a number equivalent to conservative estimates of all war-related deaths in the Middle East since the mid-1990s. That this does not shock us as it should is an indication of how we have learned to adapt to conditions that would have destabilised many other countries.

The good news is that the murder rate (measured per 100,000 people per year) has fallen from over 67 in 1994 to 31.9 in 2013, or by over 50%. However, the graphic below shows that at that level the murder rate is still 8 times higher than in the United States and almost 30 times higher than in Australia. With murder as the benchmark for public safety, South Africa remains an extraordinarily dangerous society.

Latest UN murder rate comparisons

| 1.1 | 31.9 | 3.8 |
| Australia | South Africa | United States |

The news on crime gets worse when looking at trends in key crime areas such as armed house and business robberies. Over the past decade these crime types have increased by 124% and 249% respectively. We also know from victim studies that South Africans are increasingly less inclined to report crimes to the police, and the more recent crime numbers are therefore almost certainly significant undercounts of the true extent of the criminal onslaught.

Part of the reason why crime levels remain so high is that a lot of policing policy has tended to focus on the wrong priorities. For example, for many years the police took racial and affirmative action targets more seriously than crime targets. It does not matter to anyone but the most zealous racist whether a policeman is black or white as long as she or he does the job and safeguards society. Another example of misguided priorities is the obsession South African politicians have with gun control. Thousands of man-hours and billions of rands have been wasted on bureaucracy targeting legal gun owners. Gun control is a cause politicians use to deflect public anger from the real failings of policing while

giving the public the sense that they are 'doing something' about violent crime. A stunning fact is that South Africa's armed house robbery
rate increased by over 100% after South Africa's stringent gun control
legislation was put into practice. We don't think this was because of
the new gun control laws. Rather, we use that number as an example of
how – by playing political games and focusing on the wrong priorities –
the criminal justice system fails to address the actual causes of crime.

Because crime levels are so high, and policing generally poor, South
Africans have turned away from the police and towards home-grown
community-based alternatives – and, in so doing, the state has lost the
monopoly on force in our society. The relatively wealthy middle classes
and private sector have turned to private policing on an extraordinary
scale. The graph on page 60 shows the number of private security officers
compared with the number of police officers since 1997. The numbers
started at roughly the same level of just over 110,000 in 1997, but while
the number of police officers grew modestly to 153,000, the number of
private officers rocketed to reach almost 500,000.

Poor communities did something similar, in that they too turned
away from the police. In 2016 we briefed the journalist and author Rian
Malan to conduct an investigation for the IRR into community policing
and vigilantism in poor communities in South Africa. National-level
statistics do not exist, but Malan found that most poor communities
had turned to various forms of vigilantism to protect themselves from
crime. In one area where statistics were available (Khayelitsha in Cape
Town), Malan established that more than 78 criminal suspects had been
burned and beaten to death by the community in just over a year.

It is for good reason that South Africans do not trust the police. In
2015 another IRR investigation found that the police had almost certainly been infiltrated by criminal syndicates and that police officers
were routinely involved in the planning and execution of serious and
violent crimes such as armed robberies and cash-in-transit heists. When
we presented the results of that investigation to the former Police Commissioner, Riah Phiyega, at her offices in Pretoria, she showed no

concern for the public, expressed great irritation at the results, suggested they were part of a racist conspiracy, and threatened to interdict the report. With such an attitude in the top echelon of the police, it is easy to see how the lower echelons of the police have fallen into such a parlous state of lawlessness.

Active security guards vs sworn SAPS members, 1997–2015

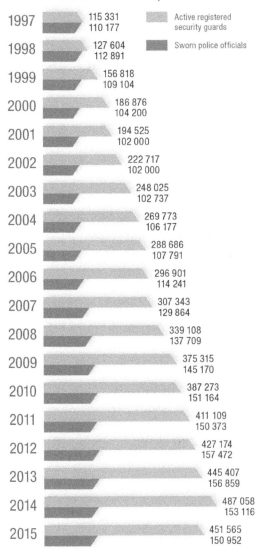

Year	Active registered security guards	Sworn police officials
1997	115 331	110 177
1998	127 604	112 891
1999	156 818	109 104
2000	186 876	104 200
2001	194 525	102 000
2002	222 717	102 000
2003	248 025	102 737
2004	269 773	106 177
2005	288 686	107 791
2006	296 901	114 241
2007	307 343	129 864
2008	339 108	137 709
2009	375 315	145 170
2010	387 273	151 164
2011	411 109	150 373
2012	427 174	157 472
2013	445 407	156 859
2014	487 058	153 116
2015	451 565	150 952

Looking back on the past twenty or so years, there have been great successes in service delivery, and living standards are much higher than they were in 1994. It is wrong to suggest that nothing has improved since 1994 or that life was better under apartheid. Real successes have been achieved even in areas usually associated with failure, such as education, crime and healthcare – and South Africans would be quite justified to reflect, briefly, with some satisfaction on what their collective efforts have achieved. But the data throws up contradictions. It is possible to 'prove', if you are so inclined, both that South Africa's education system has improved enormously and that it is one of the worst in the world. Murder rates have been cut in half, but citizens remain engaged in a low-intensity civil war against criminals. Progress in housing delivery in poor communities has been quite remarkable but is far from sufficient to meet popular expectations. The truth about progress in our living standards sits in an uncomfortable middle ground that can only be accessed if you understand the data very well and are comfortable navigating the maze of contradictions they offer up.

If you navigate back out of that maze successfully, one thing will become absolutely clear: that as expectations were ramped up, the redistributive model through which many of the successes were achieved ran out of steam. This has given rise to five distinct socio-economic risks to our future stability, ranging from the unmet expectations of young people to healthcare policy mistakes, weak family structures, electricity blackouts and water shortages, any of which could trigger something very unpleasant. The unmet expectations of young people top that list – and as long as those expectations remain unmet, South Africa will be a volatile place to live in.

Chapter 4: It all hinges on the economy

As we stare into the economic abyss, assailed by warnings of downgrades, recession, deficits and debt levels, the risk is that South Africans forget that for the first fifteen years after 1994 the economy actually performed well. This is indicated on the graph below, which tracks economic growth rates from 1981 to 2016. It measures how much new economic activity was being generated in the country and therefore the potential of the economy to support improved living conditions, generate new jobs, and generally ensure that people are better off.

Real GDP growth, 1981–2016

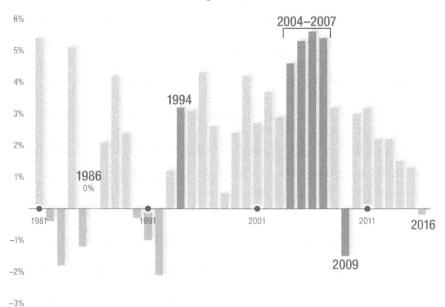

The first thing to notice is that growth rates were highly volatile in the 1980s. There were deep negative troughs and steep peaks. This was a function of uncertainty and political volatility and made it difficult to plan for the future; for that reason, foreign and local investors were uncertain about committing funds to South Africa. Uncertainty is probably the most destructive factor that can be introduced into a national economy. Good, predictable policies are the hallmark of economies that attract high levels of investment.

The second thing to notice is that growth levels were on average very low in the 1980s. South Africa spent 40% of that decade at growth rates of 0% and lower. The first three years of the 1990s all showed negative growth rates. However, growth levels stabilised in the middle and late 1990s and then began increasing quite quickly, averaging over 5% between 2004 and 2007. Those four years were very important, as two other things started to happen when growth rates approached, and then exceeded, 5%. The first is that the unemployment rate fell by almost 10 percentage points – its only sharp, sustained fall after 1994. The second is that opinion polls tracking whether people had confidence in the future of the country and also in the government hit their all-time highs at around 70%. We see a very close correlation between economic growth rates, job creation and confidence in the government, and a near-perfect correlation between the increase in the after-tax income of families and popular confidence in the future. So good is the correlation that if South Africa cannot again approach and exceed growth rates of 5%, then the unemployment crisis cannot be resolved and our future must of necessity be a volatile and unstable one.

The graph goes on to show that after 2007 things started going badly wrong. Economic growth rates fell quickly, turned negative in 2009, and have since struggled along at rates well below that of the years leading up to 2007. Much of the reason for the reversal relates to what happened at Polokwane in December of that year, when left-wing activists helped to overthrow Thabo Mbeki as leader of the ANC, which later forced his resignation as President of the country. They despised Mr Mbeki's economic policies and accused him of selling out to 'white monopoly capital' – a term used to suggest the idea that whites control the economy and use that control to actively prevent black people from becoming better off.

But black people, all people in fact, were becoming better off – the whole of chapter 3 made that point. This is indeed correct, but the anti-Mbeki activists ignored this, and even suggested the opposite, in order to justify bringing Jacob Zuma to power. Remember that both Julius Malema, who was then leader of the ANC Youth League, and Zwelinzima Vavi, who was leader of the Congress of South African Trade Unions (COSATU), were Zuma's strongest backers. They told South Africans repeatedly that if Zuma became South Africa's leader, then their lives would start to improve.

Soon after Zuma came to power as ANC leader, the party began to change South Africa's economic policy trajectory and introduced policies that did enormous damage. Examples include laws that made it more difficult to employ people, start businesses and invest in growing the economy. A proposal to expropriate private property was made. The government attempted to nationalise the private security sector. Laws were introduced to penalise businesses that did not meet racial employment targets. South African policy-makers withdrew many of the protections that had been on offer to foreign investors. The government initiated an attempt to seize the intellectual property and copyright of private firms. New travel regulations were introduced that impacted on the tourism sector. Harmful new regulations were proposed for mining firms. This list is long and created much uncertainty about whether South Africa was serious about attracting the investment necessary to grow the economy.

Unfortunately for South Africans, who reaped the consequences, the decision to abandon good economic sense coincided with the global financial crisis. The crisis was essentially triggered by the collapse of the firm Lehman Brothers in the United States in September 2008. At the time, Lehman Brothers was one of the biggest investment banks in the world. The crisis happened in part because too many subprime borrowers in the United States (those with poor credit records) had been offered mortgages that they could not possibly pay back. The term 'Ninja loans' appeared, referring to loans made to people with no income, no jobs and no assets. Financial institutions took that debt and mixed it with other products, transforming it into instruments that concealed the extent of the risk within. These they sold to each other, and soon a host of institutions were heavily exposed to this 'toxic' debt – without many analysts knowing this. When house prices collapsed the whole charade came tumbling down.

This had little to do with South Africa and we had no control over it. Our banks and lending practices were quite sound. Unfortunately, none of that matters. Trends in the global economy have as great an impact on South Africa as the domestic policy decisions we make. The following graphic shows how South Africa's economy followed global growth rates downwards, hitting a low point of –1.5% in 2009.

SA vs global economic growth, 2000–2016

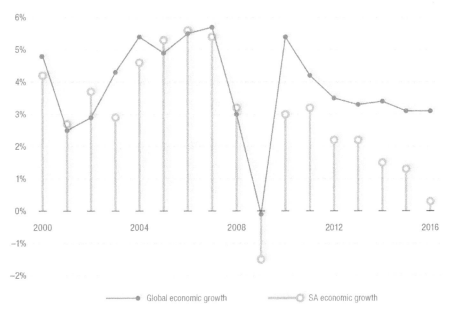

Thereafter, growth levels appeared to rebound, hitting levels of 3% and above in 2010 and 2011, but this is misleading. This apparent recovery was 'the low base effect' of the previous negative growth year; in other words, the previous year had set such a low base that it exaggerated the extent of the apparent recovery in immediately subsequent years. After 2012, as much of the contagion of the global crisis subsided, South Africa's growth rates started whittling their way down, reaching just 1.3% in 2015 and coming in at below 1% for 2016. This is very far off the 5% that is necessary to achieve the employment growth that is in turn necessary to stabilise the country.

This global growth graph is perhaps the most important in the book because it demonstrates the gap that has opened up between South African and global growth rates over the past seven or eight years. From once having closely tracked global economic performance, we now underperform. You can follow in the figure how – as global growth rates stabilised after 2011 – South Africa went into free-fall: the effect of the man-made economic catastrophe that was crafted in South Africa's cabinet by the post-2007 government.

Matters were made worse when, in the aftermath of the global crisis, the prices of commodities (iron ore, coal and copper, among others) fell very quickly. During the 2000s the world went through the top end of what is called the commodity super-cycle. The idea behind the cycle is that commodity prices are cyclical, and rise and fall like waves over very long periods of time. There is no doubt that the top-end peak was important in helping to secure the economic growth level of 5% that South Africa achieved in the middle and late 2000s. The cycle bottomed out mainly because of a change in both the rate of growth and the structure of China's economy. Between 1990 and 2010, the Chinese economy averaged growth rates approaching an incredible 10% a year. At the time, it was the world's largest consumer of commodities, which it needed to build the infrastructure of roads, bridges, dams, ports and cities to support its rapidly expanding economy. During the early 2000s China was responsible for more than half of all global steel and concrete consumption. However, China's growth rate began to slow. Between 2010 and 2015 the Chinese economic growth rate slipped year after year to bottom out at rates of around 6%. As growth fell, China's demand for commodities began to fall, and so prices fell.

This mattered for South Africa, as commodities were such a substantial export product. When the world's biggest buyer of those products started buying less, the export economy took a significant knock. It did not help, of course, that politicians were at the same time threatening to nationalise South Africa's mining industry and introduce taxes that had the potential to push it into bankruptcy.

In a conversation I had with an ANC leader and former trade unionist in 2016, the point was made that if South Africa can ride out the current price trough and wait for the next peak, then our economy may automatically start to look a lot better. This could be true, but for three reservations. The first is that not enough has been done to renew confidence in South Africa as a mining investment destination. Therefore, even if prices pick up again, that cycle may pass South Africa by. The second is that commodity prices at the top end of the 2000s super-cycle peak were out of all proportion to those of previous peaks. Therefore, even if commodity prices again rebound, they may not rebound to the levels at which they were before. The third is a set of reservations that all relate to China. Chinese demand drives the super-cycle. But that also means that China becomes a victim of the cycle in having to pay very high peak prices. At present China is growing more slowly. It may take many years for it to grow into the excess infrastructure it has built and consume the commodity stockpiles that exist. It may therefore be learning to moderate its demand in order to moderate prices. Whereas miners had been price-setters and China a price-taker, that relationship may now have been reversed. China's east coast middle class is also taking off. Some estimates see it growing from 50 million people two decades ago to over 400 million in 2030. Satellite photographs taken at night over the past twenty years show the east coast literally lighting up. This means that China can change the nature of growth in its economy, away from the massive infrastructure (and therefore commodity-consuming) growth of the past two decades, to a model of more internally focused consumer-led growth. This may keep commodity prices lower for longer than many analysts expect. For all these reservations, caution is warranted around the idea that South Africa can simply wait out the commodity price slump.

India is, however, worth watching closely to see whether it will in time take up some of the global commodity slack. So too whether the United States and some European governments (and maybe Japan) launch into long-term infrastructure investment programmes over the next decade. Such outcomes may contribute to an unexpected yet welcome boost for South African commodity exporters.

The combined effect of the post-Polokwane policy shifts, the subprime crisis in the United States and the global commodity downturn was too much for the South African economy to withstand. It was the worst combination of forces the country could possibly have experienced.

The consequences are something that all South Africans felt quite directly – they stopped getting richer. In the graph below we track GDP per capita from 1981 onwards. What this means is that we are taking the total production of the economy and dividing it among all the people in South Africa. We are starting in 1981 because that was the year in which real (inflation-adjusted) per capita GDP historically peaked at a level of just over R50,000 per person.

GDP per capita, 1981–2016

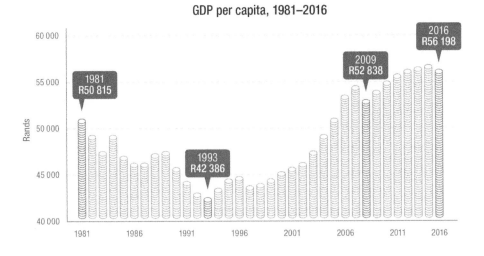

During the volatility of the 1980s South Africans got poorer. You can follow in the graph how per capita GDP levels fell to reach just over R40,000 per head in 1993. Thereafter, as the mostly sensible economic policies of the ANC government took effect, and economic growth increased, South Africans started getting richer again. In 2006, precisely 25 years after the previous 1981 peak, South Africans were on average again as rich as they had been 25 years before – the price paid for the poor policy decisions and political volatility of the 1970s and 1980s. The upward trend in per capita GDP was interrupted only by the global financial crisis, after which, as growth levels again declined, per capita GDP stagnated. That stagnation is the legacy that South Africa's post-2007 government has bequeathed – it took an economy that was creating jobs and making people richer and in just a few years turned it into an economy in which people are getting poorer.

The economic outlook becomes more difficult when factoring in the risk that the hard gains on other economic indicators, most notably interest rates and bond yields, may now also be surrendered. The graph below tracks interest rate levels from the 1980s into 2015. It shows how

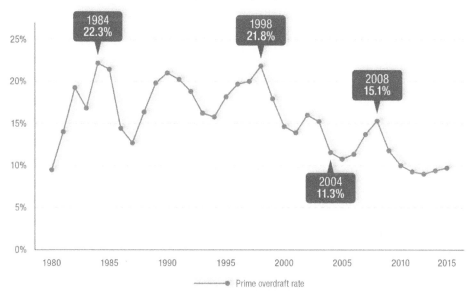

Interest rates, 1980–2015

Prime overdraft rate

rates that were at levels of over 20% were cut in half. The result was to make it easier and cheaper for business people and the middle classes to borrow the money they needed to start new enterprises or buy homes, cars and other goods. Their living standards therefore increased and the economy benefited from growing economic activity.

South Africa is now at the beginning of a new interest-rate hike cycle. Such hikes may be forced on the country both in an effort to moderate inflation and to ensure the broadest possible interest-rate differential between South Africa, on the one hand, and the United States and Europe, on the other. This is necessary in order to manage the flow of speculative yield seeking investment into our country, which is investment that takes money out of economies with very low interest rates and invests it in those with higher returns. Because our export performance is so weak, we need those inflows in order to finance our imports. If Western central bankers start raising rates, they will force us to do the same. But the effect of raising rates will reduce consumer spending and place a great many households under increased economic pressure. Black middle-class households especially, as a first-generation middle class, will find it very difficult to service the debt they have incurred to reach the middle classes. As interest rates increased from the lows reached in and around 2005 to break through the 15% level in 2008, the debt level of households expressed as a proportion of their disposable income began to rise very fast. Levels of unsecured lending are growing faster than levels of secured lending – a further indication of stressed households having to borrow money just to get through each month.

In the late 1990s and early 2000s, as interest rates were falling and economic growth increased, bond yields were also declining – but the risk is that those yields will now also increase. Governments need money, and there are essentially two sources they can access. The first is revenue from taxation. The second is by borrowing the money. They often borrow by issuing bonds which investors can buy. The bond holder is paid interest by the government on that bond. The graph on page 71 shows how yields on government ten-year bonds in South Africa have fallen over the past two decades.

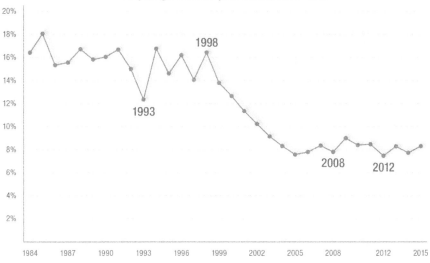

10-year government yield bonds, 1984–2015

The reason for the fall is that the yield includes a measure of the risk associated with the country or society offering the bond. In the 1990s South Africa was perceived as a very high-risk investment, hence the high yields – to justify the risk, you needed to get a very high return on the money being invested in the government. As the society stabilised and the future began to look more positive, so bond yields fell. This was a very good thing, as it allowed the government to borrow more cheaply in order to invest in infrastructure, for example. The danger now is that yields will again increase as the risk equation for South Africa worsens. It will cost the government more to borrow the money it needs to develop infrastructure such as schools, roads and hospitals, and it will be forced to develop less infrastructure, resulting in lower economic growth and fewer jobs.

The post-2007 government has already thrown away what was arguably our greatest economic strength of all – and also perhaps the ANC's most impressive achievement in government. This was the extent to which it reduced the debt levels of the government in its first fifteen years in office. The following graph shows what is called the debt-to-GDP ratio of the government (and measures this against the economic growth rate of the economy). This is a measure of total government debt divided by GDP. The state is required to pay interest on the debt, so by reducing the debt it frees up money that can be spent on other things, such as building schools or roads – or paying social grants. The graph depicts how debt levels declined from near 50% of GDP in 1994 to below 30% by mid-2008.

Growth and public debt, 1994–2016

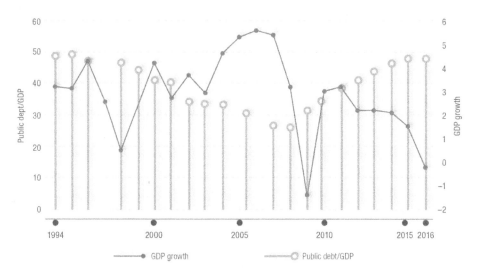

The resultant savings on the interest bill of the government made possible much of the social development and welfare spending of the past twenty years. However, after 2007 growth levels declined sharply and a desperate government started borrowing more and more money to keep financing its social development programme and other areas of expenditure. The result was that debt levels again began to increase. Within just five or six years the government had undone all the progress made since 1994 and debt levels were back to where they had been at the end of apartheid. The data in the graph excludes guarantees made to parastatals, so the actual debt level is even higher. Higher interest payments on that debt take money away from welfare programmes, for example, and all people, poor people especially, are left very much worse off. It is a recipe for disaster, but it is also an unfortunately familiar pattern that has played itself out under a host of recent leftist govern-ments, from Venezuela and Zimbabwe to Brazil.

The result of the relative growth–debt reversal is that the government is running out of money and this is making it dangerous and unpredict-able. Its tax base is very small. Of 33 million adults, only 5–6 million pay personal income tax. About half a million people pay upwards of half of all income tax. These are the same people who run the companies that pay corporate tax and that generate the economic activity that makes VAT receipts possible. They represent a small, mobile upper-middle class, and if the government makes their lives too difficult they, their money and their businesses may leave the country, triggering a tax crisis for the government, in that its expenditure will significantly exceed its rev-enues. That is already happening to some extent.

In the following graph there are two lines. The one represents the total revenue (or income) of the government expressed as a proportion of GDP. The other is the total expenditure of the government.

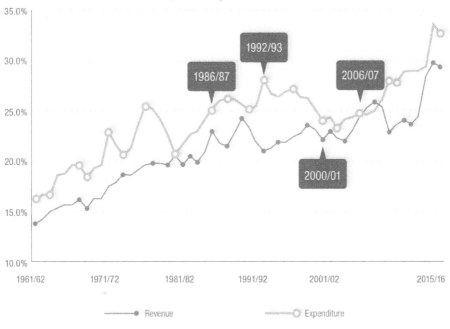

Government revenue and expenditure
as a percentage of GDP, 1961–2016

When the government came to power in 1994, it inherited a considerable gap between its income and its expenditure. As growth levels increased and debt levels (and therefore interest payments) fell, that gap closed and in two years the government even recorded surpluses – earning more in revenue than it spent, which allowed it to save some of the difference for future needs. After 2007, the gap between revenue and expenditure again widened. With higher debt levels, likely increased bond yields and low economic growth, the government is going to keep running out of money. It is spending far more than it earns and it is likely to find itself in precisely the same trouble that you or I would get into if we ran our household finances in the same way.

When leftist governments run out of money, they typically do one of two things. The first is to print lots of money, as Robert Mugabe did in Zimbabwe. The result is that inflation increases very quickly and this reduces the value of that money. People lose their investments and pensions, and soon the whole country is impoverished. South Africa has not started doing this, at least not yet. The second thing leftist governments do is to start confiscating things such as businesses, homes, farms and the money in people's bank accounts and savings. There is a concerning degree of evidence that the government is considering this. My policy colleagues have tracked and lobbied against an estimated thirteen relatively new laws and policies that would allow the government to seize privately held assets. The ministers who are pushing for these laws are doing so because, even though they won't admit it yet, they know that their economic policies are failing people. They know they have got it wrong and that the policy changes they introduced after 2007 are making people poorer. They also know that their policies will never work and they are afraid of the consequences. So they are positioning themselves so that when the angry mob arrives at their door, they can try to placate it for a time with offers of 'free' farms, money, homes, businesses and other property – if it comes to that.

While a lot went right in the economy in the years from 1994 to 2007, there were shortcomings. Perhaps the most important of these related to jobs and labour-market policy. The next graphic tracks economic growth against the unemployment rate from 1994 to 2016. It shows that the unemployment rate has not changed much from around 35%, despite the fact that the number of people with jobs doubled over the same years. In other words, despite creating large numbers of jobs, insufficient jobs were created to meet demand.

GDP growth vs unemployment rate, 1994–2016

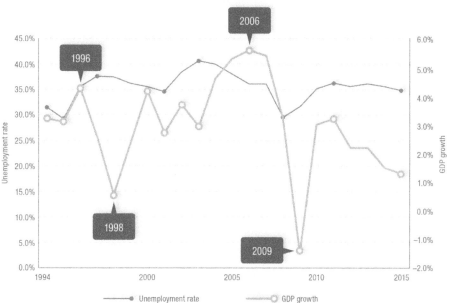

On average, South Africa has created approximately 375,000 net new jobs per year since 1994. As a guiding rule, we create just over 100,000 net new jobs per point of GDP growth per year. Yet if we set the goal of raising black employment rates to match white employment rates, this will require doubling the number of black people with a job – or creating around 1,000,000 net new jobs per year for the next decade. Anything less is to condemn significant numbers of people to another decade without work. It can be done, but only with growth rates of around 7%–8% in an environment of significant labour-market liberalisation.

We know that the great majority of people who do not have jobs are young and poorly educated. There is a number called the labour market absorption rate that measures what percentage of people of working age have a job. For South Africa the figure is 43%, which is very much below that of most comparable emerging markets. There is also a correlation between the labour-market absorption rate and a person's level of education. For people with no formal education, the labour-market absorption rate is around 30%. For people with primary- or some high-school education, it is between 40% and 50%. However, for those with a good degree from a good university, the rate increases to above 80%.

Highly skilled people in South Africa therefore find work quite easily, while less-skilled people do not. In all the scenario briefings we have delivered in recent years, we have not come across one enterprise that is aggressively hiring unskilled people. The opposite is more often true. Employers are nervous of hiring workers because of the destructive behaviour of many trade unions and because of the risk and administrative burden associated with South Africa's labour laws. International benchmark studies rank South Africa's labour policy environment as one of the most restrictive. These laws have made the broader cost of labour (not just wage levels, but the complete administrative and other costs of employing someone) too great relative to the value that a young unskilled worker would provide to the business in question. The price for this situation is paid by poor and unskilled people, who cannot find work and remain dependent on welfare.

Pointless proposals are often made, such as new minimum wages, with people suggesting that these will help job creation. Other than the inference that laws of supply and demand do not apply to labour markets, these proposals ignore the fact that, regardless of what the government 'declares', the real minimum wage will always be R0 per month, as that is what the unemployed earn. As long as the cost of labour exceeds its productive value, great numbers of South Africans will remain unemployed.

South Africa finds itself in a position where welfare and service delivery progress have meant that living standards increased in poor communities, but at the same time labour laws meant that too few people in those communities were finding the jobs they would need to continue improving their own standards of living. The clash between low labour-market absorption rates and quickly increasing living standards created the crisis of rising expectations with which we concluded the previous chapter. The counterproductive effect of labour market policy was further exacerbated by government policy in areas such as mining, manufacturing, tourism and agriculture, which deterred investment in the sectors most likely to provide work to poor and relatively unskilled people.

The effects of misguided and inept labour market policy were further exacerbated by militant trade union activity. Data produced by the labour market analyst Andrew Levy shows that in the late 1970s and early 1980s the number of man-days lost as a result of strike action rarely exceeded 1 million (a man-day is lost if one worker strikes for one day). However, in the late 1980s and into the mid-1990s, as the democratic settlement was being negotiated, man-days lost spiked, hitting approximately 9 million in 1987, over 3 million in 1989, and over 4 million in 1990 and again in 1992. In the immediate post-settlement era, strike action flattened out, and in the ten years between 1995 and 2004 man-days lost exceeded 2 million on only two occasions. However, in the run-up to the fractious 2007 ANC policy conference that ended the political career of Thabo Mbeki, strike action spiked again. In that particular year a staggering 12.9 million man-days were lost. That record was beaten, however, two years later in 2010 when the newly triumphant, and union-backed, administration of Jacob Zuma set about swinging policy in South Africa to the left. In three of the subsequent four years, trade union activity saw man-days lost exceed 5 million a year. This caused further damage to investor perceptions of South Africa, and in our own scenario work we saw a definite trend of firms turning away from the idea of employing low-skilled labour.

Some of the damage caused by misguided labour policy and trade union action can be measured by an indicator called the structure of GDP. This measures how much specific industries contribute to the economy. The manufacturing industry has seen its share of GDP fall by almost half, from 23% to 13%, since 1994. That of agriculture has fallen from 4.5% to 2.4%, and that of mining has remained flat at around 9% to 10%, despite the decline in the real effective exchange rate. The one sector that really took off is the high-tech, high-skilled services economy – yet this happened in a country where far too few people receive the education necessary to find work in such skilled professions.

The data shows a distinct trend of deindustrialisation. Presiding over this trend was perhaps the ANC's greatest economic policy failure, as it helped to foster the economy's commodity export dependence, which was unmasked when global commodity prices fell. The deindustrialisation trend is confirmed when we measure how many jobs exist in each economic sector. Between 1994 and 2015 the number of jobs in manufacturing fell by 276,000 or almost 20%, from 1,409,977 to 1,134,000, and in mining by 110,000, or 18%, from around 600,000 to around 490,000. In the services economy, meanwhile, the number of jobs increased from 2,066,258 to 4,936,000, or by 139%.

To make labour-market matters more complicated, the government has also been 'cheating' since 2008 with South Africa's unemployment rate and jobs numbers. You will recall that the unemployment rate has hovered at around 35% since 1994. You may also have noticed that after the economy began to crash in 2008, there was no increase in the unemployment rate. The reason is that as the private sector stopped creating jobs, the government started employing people at a significant rate. Over the last decade the number of people working for the government increased from roughly 1.5 million to over 2 million. This helped create the illusion that the unemployment rate was not increasing (while also creating the somewhat artificial sense that individual income tax revenues were growing). As we have also seen in rising government debt levels and the increasing budget deficit, the government was essentially borrowing the money it used to pay these people. That this cannot possibly be sustained has yet to be understood in some quarters. Late in 2016 a senior civil servant, seemingly irritated by our diagnosis of South Africa's economic slump, suggested that if the economy were to slip into recession, and the private sector retrenched large numbers of workers, the state could just employ them – so what is the problem?

The case for recession draws much strength from what is happening deep within the mining, manufacturing, and consumer economies. The graphic below tracks year-on-year changes in mining production for South Africa since January 2011. It shows that the sector has struggled to maintain production levels for much of the past six or seven years and that the industry has been trapped in a steeply negative trend since March 2015.

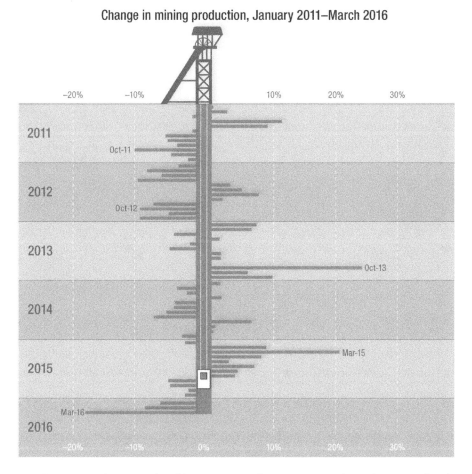

Change in mining production, January 2011–March 2016

This is partly a result of low commodity prices and partly a result of what remains an unstable and unfriendly set of mining investment policies. Any analysis must also take into account that the government has for several years dragged its feet in doing what it knows will have to be done to attract new mining investment to South Africa. Cynical analysts suggest that the government is intentionally harming the industry in an effort to force existing miners out so that corrupt politicians and their cronies can buy up mining assets through taxpayer-funded 'empowerment' deals.

Manufacturing is in just as much trouble as mining – and, again, just as little is being done to help the industry. The graph below tracks changes in South Africa's manufacturing production index. The index was weighted to 100 points in 2010. It has struggled since then to keep ahead of that 100-point mark, showing that it is not expanding and the short-term trend on the index is a sharp contraction.

Weighted Manufacturing Production Index
2010 = 100

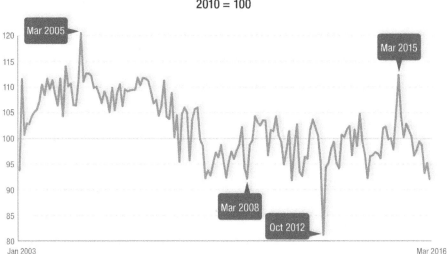

Reasons include rising domestic costs such as electricity, rising labour costs and volatility, imports from more competitive manufacturing economies, increased consumer debt levels, and of course the great burden that is placed on South African entrepreneurs through the enormous compliance demands of the government's various racial empowerment rules.

Consumers who drive the domestic economy are in even greater trouble than miners and manufacturers. Consumers matter because the consumption expenditure of households is equivalent to almost 60% of GDP. The next graph tracks that expenditure against economic growth and a third indicator called the consumer confidence index. This index tracks whether consumers are inclined to spend money. The graph shows a near-perfect relationship between the three indicators. As confidence increases, so do expenditure and growth, and vice versa. In the global financial crisis years, confidence fell sharply, then recovered (the low base effect), and has subsequently hit decade-deep lows. That alone is sufficient to raise doubt about the prospects for a short- or medium-term South African economic recovery. Add the prospects for rising interest rates, and household consumption expenditure is likely to remain depressed for longer than many analysts predict.

Consumer spending, consumer confidence and GDP growth, 2000–2016

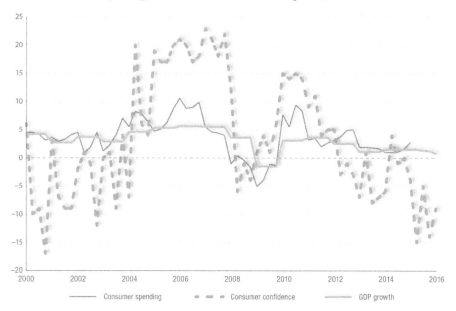

The economic picture that emerges from all this is not a very healthy one. The economist John Loos makes the point that South Africa has exhausted all the easy economic options that were open to it or, as he puts it, has 'pulled all the easy levers'. The end of sanctions and opening up of the economy to the world was one such lever that gave the economy a significant boost – the benefit of which has now run its course. Cutting interest rates in half was a second lever, as a result of which the economy, for a time, grew very strongly as previously untapped consumer spending was unleashed. But that era, too, has come to an end. The third lever came as bond yields were cut in half – but ratings downgrades will reverse that trend. The freebie of high commodity prices has also run its course.

All four levers helped the ANC to bring the economic growth rate up to 5%. But all four have now been exhausted, and there are no easy levers left to pull. Only the tough options remain, such as labour-market reform, mass privatisation, securing property rights, and cutting the costs inherent in South Africa's empowerment policies.

Even if the remaining growth levers are pulled, we must also factor in the risk to our economy of record-high stock markets stuffed full of quantitative easing money, new mortgage debt crises in the United States, a stuttering European recovery, and the potential for a global banking crisis and for a Chinese housing bubble. Add to that the impact of technology that will increasingly come to do the jobs that people once did, and, if anything, the economic risk equation for South Africa is vastly understated.

That we are probably going to remain in a degree of economic trouble for some time to come is a story confirmed, and best told, in the single most useful measure of where South Africa is headed – the leading indicator of the Reserve Bank. The indicator is a composite index indicative of future economic growth. If the indicator is picking up, then growth is liable to pick up. If it is falling, then expect economic growth rates to fall.

The following graph depicts the relationship between the lead indicator and the economic growth rate all the way back to 1960. It is a near-perfect predictor for economic growth. Every peak in the indicator brought about a peak in the economic growth rate, and vice versa. One can see very clearly the deep dive in the indicator that accompanied the global financial crisis and, again, the apparent recovery and thereafter the now-familiar downward trajectory since 2010.

Lead indicator and GDP growth, 1960–2016

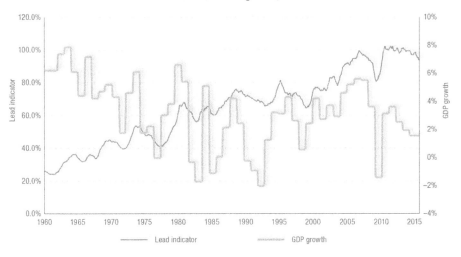

Run your eye back down the indicator, and you will see that South Africa was last in a slump comparable to that of today from the late 1980s into the mid-1990s. The circumstances for the slump, if you want to give them a milestone in time, were set by two events in August 1985 – firstly, the Rubicon speech in which P.W. Botha defiantly stated, in the face of economic and political reality, that his government would not reform; and, secondly, the decision of the American banking group Chase Manhattan not to extend further loans to South Africa. The slump drew more impetus from the 'Black Monday' stock-market crash of October 1987 and the ensuing global recession, together with deepening internal political conflict and uncertainty before bottoming out in the aftermath of the 1997 Asian financial crisis – having rallied between 1991 and 1995 on the positive sentiment generated by the release of Nelson Mandela and South Africa's transition negotiations. The indicator showed a very positive trajectory improvement from the late 1990s up to the 2009 global crisis, as improved global circumstances coincided with broadly sensible domestic policy. A coincidence of both those circumstances will be necessary to support another decade of economic recovery.

It is an indictment of the South African government that came to power after the Polokwane conference in 2007 that it has, in just a few short years, undone so much of the positive economic progress that South Africa made in its first fifteen years as a democracy. The critical mistake was to allow growth levels to plummet as debt levels increased. The model of gradually rising levels of economic growth and shrewd, conservative fiscal management would in all likelihood, had it continued, been sufficient to position South Africa as a prosperous middle-income economy by the early 2030s. But now a lot of that progress has been undermined and the outlook could easily be for even more economic hardship that will trigger greater political and social instability.

As in the 1980s, it will take reforms to current policy to avert that outcome and turn the leading indicator upwards again. As in the 1980s and 1990s, the reforms need to amount to a fundamental reworking of the policy environment. An approach that seeks rather to tinker with policies that have already failed, in the hope of achieving much-improved economic results, cannot possibly succeed.

Chapter 5: The race war cometh

Only slightly more frightening than the state of the economy is the prospect of a race war. If you read the newspapers or follow social media, you could be forgiven for thinking that the war could break out tomorrow. Various commentators have made predictions of purges and pogroms and talk about the incredible race rage in the country. They warn that if more is not done to redistribute wealth, that racial rage will explode into violence. Their dire predictions draw much apparent veracity from the plague of destruction and violence that plays out on South Africa's television screens every evening – notwithstanding the efforts of the South African Broadcasting Corporation (SABC) to shield the public from having to view such mayhem. Municipal offices, police stations, university buildings and schools are looted and set alight by crowds of young protesters. Police officers engage daily in running battles with youthful activists – the police firing gas and rubber bullets while the protesters respond with stones and insults.

It is true that the levels of political protest are escalating. Data we receive from the police shows that over the past decade the number of violent anti-government protests has more than doubled. Since 2015 we have seen the sharpest increase on record. We believe that the police number is almost certainly an undercount – not because the police are hiding anything, but rather because the sheer volume of protests is so overwhelming. We also believe that the number of protests will continue to increase, developing a strong racial flavour, becoming more violent, and that they will seek out ever more prominent targets in the government and the private sector. To some extent this has already happened.

When the protest movement really got going about a decade ago, protests tended to be about local issues and occurred sporadically in small towns and poor townships around the country. Especially since 2014 that has changed. Protests have started to become about national issues, such as university fees, and corruption, such as that around the President's homestead at Nkandla – not just about localised service delivery shortcomings here or there. Protesters are also starting to identify more prominent targets. Marching to some dusty local government office no longer makes the headlines. But when university students stormed the Union Buildings in late 2015, that made global network news headlines. So, too, when students broke through the gates of Parliament in that same year and briefly occupied the square in front of the parliamentary building. Their 2016 invasion of the offices of the Higher Education Department and subsequent march to the Chamber of Mines show the same trend.

Protests are also developing an odious racial character. Protest leaders are often guilty of the crudest form of race baiting and racial nationalist incitement. When almost 80% of students at the University of the Witwatersrand voted to return to class in late 2016, the protest leaders said the vote revealed the racism of white students and a message was circulated calling for the killing of white students. *F&#$ the whites* was a slogan seen on T-shirts worn by student protesters and shouted in lecture theatres. When warnings were issued of the harm being caused to higher education, the protest leaders responded that this showed how whites dominated the university community.

What is more alarming is the casual manner in which protesters resort to violence and destruction of property when they don't get what they want, confident in the knowledge that their behaviour is unlikely to result in criminal charges – as it should in any country where law and order is taken seriously. If you don't get what you want, then burn something to get the attention of the government and the media. If you get what you want, then burn it anyway.

A police general explained how every time his officers are deployed to quell one of these violent uprisings, he hears the same story. The politicians made wild promises, failed to keep them, and all too often misappropriated the funds meant for the issue in question. The community sought to complain, but the relevant local, provincial or national political leadership either ignored them or promised to follow up but never did. Exposed to this kind of indifference for years, the local community, inspired by the images of mayhem broadcast from other corners of the country, decide to cause their own mayhem in a bid to attract national media attention. With a nonchalance that borders on the cavalier, the politicians then send the police in to restore order – as if they are some magical force whose stun grenades and rubber bullets can make up for years of political indifference. Few commentators have sufficient understanding of, or sympathy for, the impossible position in which the police are being placed. They have neither the numbers nor proper riot policing resources to keep up with what the politicians are demanding of them – as that same general, somewhat ominously, warned, 'we are not Plan B to govern the country'.

Part of the reason why race-tinged violence is becoming commonplace in protest action is that various commentators and activists legitimise it. It truly is frightening to read some of the things that are written – not by drunken louts but by educated people in what one might have thought were respectable publications. Lectures are held at universities, the transcripts of which read like a throwback to Germany in November of 1938. When a university building is burned to the ground, media commentators write reams about the emotional pain that must have driven the students to embark upon such an act of vandalism. This is nonsense. Arrest the vandals and tell the rest to grow up. In a civilised society, if the government of the day does not listen to you, then you vote for another government. South Africans get that opportunity every two and a half years on average in either local or national and provincial polls. That they choose not to use that political tool can in no way justify resorting to violence. Where will it end if 'feeling unhappy' is sufficient justification for arson? The entire country will be burned to the ground.

Matters are, of course, not helped when some members of Parliament turn the National Assembly into a scene of mayhem, complete with fisticuffs and the hurling of profanities and racial insults across the floor. Mangosuthu Buthelezi got it absolutely right when he stood up in Parliament, amid one of the melees, and pleaded with the Speaker to stop what he so wonderfully described as this 'poppycock'. Jonathan Jansen was also correct when he described the behaviour of many protesters as 'vulgar'. We have in our possession a letter that Nelson Mandela wrote to us as a young man seeking a bursary to complete his legal studies. It is beautifully written and argued. Comparing it with the racist rantings and exhortations to anarchy that pass as 'youth leadership' in much of the country today is both frightening and depressing. If this is the calibre of our future leadership, what horrors lie in wait?

It would seem quite accurate, then, for the news media and social media to tell a story of a society that is gripped by hatred and loathing and where race relations have reached a low point since 1994. Read enough and you will come away certain that racial hatred and resentment are literally hard-wired into the South African DNA. We are told that whites are resentful of blacks and want to go back to the apartheid days. Whites apparently care nothing for the country and are racists of the worst order. On the other side of spectrum, it is common to hear that black people are equally resentful of whites and wish to drive them all into the sea, or worse.

Not without some trepidation we decided to find out what people actually think through a nationally representative field survey. The results, released in 2016, were so inspiring that we titled the report that accompanied their release *Race Relations in South Africa: Reasons for Hope*.

We asked South Africans to identify what they saw as the two most serious problems not yet resolved since 1994. The top two issues so identified were unemployment and crime. In total, 55.9% of South Africans saw unemployment as the most pressing problem, while 28.8% cited crime. Racism was cited by just 4.7% of respondents. Keep in mind that these responses were not prompted and that respondents were free to list any issue that was important to them.

We then asked people whether race relations had improved since 1994.

The majority of respondents (54%) thought that this was so. Just under a quarter of respondents (22.2%) said that race relations had stayed the same, while only one in five South Africans (20.4%) felt they had become worse. In the report that accompanied the release of the polling results we wrote, 'Hence, the impression that has been created in the media and on social media – that race relations have worsened sharply – does not square with the views of South Africans themselves.'

We pushed even deeper into the really tough, super-controversial, racial questions, such as those about redress, affirmative action and quotas in sports. We asked, 'Who do you think should be appointed to jobs in South Africa?' and gave respondents a series of options to choose from. Only 4.7% of people supported the first option, that 'only black people should be appointed to jobs for a very long time ahead'. Only 5.8% of people supported our second option, that 'only black people should be appointed until those in employment are demographically representative'. The overwhelming view, shared by 70% of South Africans, was that appointments should be based on merit, but that real efforts should at the same time be made to help previously disadvantaged people.

We then pressed further, asking whether South African sports teams should be selected 'only by merit and ability and not by racial quotas'. The government would later ban rugby and cricket codes from hosting international sports competitions on the grounds that South Africans were outraged that more had not been done to meet racial quotas. Rugby and cricket authorities would subsequently justify strict racial quotas on the basis that this was what South Africans wanted. To use Buthelezi's term, it is all poppycock. Survey responses showed that 77% of all South Africans support purely merit-based selections without reference to racial quotas. No fewer than 74.2% of black South Africans endorsed this view.

When we looked more closely at the results, it was remarkable that 13% of coloured people, 15.1% of white people and 25.5% of black people were open to the use of quotas. This showed that while opinions are clearly split, they are split within racial groups rather than between them, which is one of the most important insights into South Africa's race relations.

What people want for their children is a deeply personal issue. It is thus a very good basis to test their real beliefs about race relations. We asked parents whether they would support their children being taught by a school teacher of another race. In an answer that should fill us with renewed courage to face the future, 90.8% of South Africans said it did not matter what race their children's teachers were. For black people, the figure was 91.9%, for coloured people 90.6%, for Asian people 99.1%, and for white people 80.6%. Admittedly, this meant that the race of a teacher matters to 2 in 10 white South African parents (and to 1 in 10 coloured and black people). But that it does not matter to the other 8 or 9 out of 10 people is more important. Too often the media defines race relations in terms of what the 1 in 10 or 2 in 10 South Africans think or say. We prefer to define the real state of race relations in terms of what the 8 in 10 think, which is why it was distressing to learn that one media editor had issued instructions banning any reports of the study.

We also wanted to know what South Africans think needs to be done to promote sound future race relations. We therefore asked if people thought that better education and more jobs, the building blocks for every successful society, would make socio-economic differences between races steadily disappear. The responses showed that 82.2% of South Africans agreed. Only 7.2% of South Africans disagreed. The proportion of black people who agreed (82.8%) was approximately the same as the proportion of white people (81.7%), again showing a coincidence of views across racial lines on important issues. This in turn supports much of our earlier analysis that South Africa's future stability will be decided in the economy.

Finally, we wanted to know whether South Africans understand and value their mutual interdependence and want full opportunities for all. In a result from which we should draw even greater fortitude, 85.4% of all South Africans agreed that 'the different races need each other and there should be full opportunity for people of all races'. Only 5.7% of black people, 5.2% of coloured people, 3.1% of Asian people and 4.9% of white people disagreed.

Our conclusions were that, despite tough economic conditions and unmet expectations, race relations remain sound. The quiet majority of South Africans respect each other and want to work together to build a better country. That this is so is, of course, not a reason for complacency. Quite the opposite is true. More than a decade ago, when we conducted a similar survey, we also found that race relations had generally improved since 1994 and that black and white South Africans were well aware that they needed each other to make progress. The late IRR president, and South Africa's greatest social scientist, Professor Lawrence Schlemmer, warned that politicians and other commentators might seek to foment racial divisions for political or ideological gain. Moreover, the more the economy faltered and unemployment grew, the easier this would be to achieve. Be further mindful of the warning of a senior South Africa analyst, with a track record of being right on many issues, who remarked about our survey that generally good race relations would probably also have been true of Zimbabwe before the land invasions. It thus takes only a small handful of sinister individuals to turn a country against itself and promote violent pandemonium.

How are they able to do that? Why, if South Africans respect each other, agree on what it will take to build a better country, and remain so firmly committed to working together, does the impression take hold that they are set against each other? Much of the reason relates to a combination of manufactured outrage and the cynical manipulation of legitimate social and economic causes in order to pursue unrelated political and ideological goals.

Off the record, several university vice-chancellors say that the protests on their campuses were not a spontaneous display of student frustrations but rather an orchestrated manipulation of student frustrations to pursue unrelated ideological and political goals. Officials in the Western Cape government say that many of the larger-scale protests that swept the province have the same hallmarks. Senior ANC leaders are convinced that some of the larger-scale protests directed at their party have been orchestrated in a similar manner. It is well understood in the mining industry that there was a lot more to the uprising at Marikana than the frustrations of mine workers. The State Security Agency believes that these orchestrated efforts at causing turmoil and racial division are driven by the loosest of coalitions of ultra-leftist dissidents, many with former roots in the ANC (and some embedded journalists and academics) who are for the most part financed by naive development agencies that believe their partners' professed intentions to address pressing social and economic problems. The strategy for sowing mayhem and division is alleged to have three components.

The first is to manufacture and foster a sense of desperation and anger within poorer communities by denying the real social and economic progress the country has made over the past twenty years and, instead, telling a story of how ruthlessly exploited the poor remain, that nothing got better after 1994, that Nelson Mandela and the ANC sold out, that the middle classes have grown grotesquely rich at the expense of the poor, and that only violent revolution and a reversal of the negotiated settlement of the 1990s, complete with the rejection of the constitutional framework, can liberate the poor from poverty. Often these arguments are expressed in racial terms to suggest that the relative prosperity of the white middle classes is directly responsible for black poverty and that the prosperity of one race needs to be destroyed before the other can be prosperous. These arguments are put out in the news media and social media with growing regularity.

The second component is to discredit both the DA and the ANC in the eyes of prospective voters. The aim here is to create the idea that South Africa cannot improve within the confines of the current political or parliamentary system. These arguments are also often set in racial terms, for example, that the political opposition is there to defend 'white wealth' and that the ANC sold out to 'white monopoly capital'.

The third component is to actively engineer incidents of conflict and violent protest between citizens and the state. Clashes can then be used as examples of state-sponsored violence in order to further question the legitimacy of the state, cultivate a deeper sense of persecution, and more effectively reinforce the message that the poor are actively oppressed by a corrupt state that is conspiring with a racist private sector and business community.

What does the evidence say?

Consider a typical example. An incident of racism is alleged, such as a fight in the parking lot of a nightclub. A small group of activists will raise that incident to the level of a national emergency – complete with warnings of race wars, Mandela selling out, and generally that social relations have reached a point of no return. It is suggested that all people of the other race are rapists/murderers/thieves or similar. When that provocation elicits the inevitable backlash, that backlash is then employed for days on end in an effort to incite tensions and promote divisions in the society – these are then presented as evidence of the failure of the capitalist system and the need to remove the government of the day. That is quite a leap – a bar fight taken all the way to the need to defeat capitalism and unseat the government.

Or take the example of university fees. Many students struggle to pay their fees and to afford board and lodging at university. The students are organised, funded and marshalled to challenge the government to do something to help them. But months later, the students are in a worse position, while their campaign has morphed, under their noses, into another campaign to unseat the capitalist system and the ANC – complete with the now-familiar race-baiting incitement. When genuine efforts are made to help the students, these are sabotaged. More than that, extensive violence has occurred, including violence directed at the very university managers who are undoubtedly on the side of the students and want to help them solve their problems. Vehicles and property are burned. Students are assaulted in lecture theatres. When desperate university managers reluctantly call on the police for assistance, the violence is then blamed on the 'militarisation of campuses' by the police and university managers – as though scores of hardworking students were just peacefully going to the library when the police opened fire on them.

Take a third example. Residents of the Western Cape's poorer towns demand better housing and sanitation. They are also funded, marshalled and bused to a protest. Fiery speeches are made about the need for 'war' and violent revolution. Alcohol flows freely and when emotions have been truly riled up, the protesting crowd is released onto the streets and the inevitable clash with the police plays out on television. But weeks later, those community demands for housing and better sanitation have also morphed, again under their noses, into demands to unseat the government of the Western Cape and bring an end to capitalism.

This was the same demand ultimately reached by the Rhodes Must Fall movement, which – after Rhodes fell – morphed into the Fees Must Fall movement, which, if the pattern is to be repeated, will morph over and over again into new and eventually impossible demands.

Readers can draw their own conclusions, but it seems unlikely that four such distinct campaigns could coincidentally settle on precisely the same two demands – and, more than that, they are demands that have very little to do with the issues that originally gave rise to each campaign. Furthermore, as each campaign was exposed to critical scrutiny, it turned to racist incitement in an attempt to deflect tough and legitimate questions. But this is not unique to South Africa. Look closely at the Occupy Wall Street and, more recently, the Black Lives Matter campaigns in the United States, and the same pattern is evident – the exploitation of (at times) legitimate community concerns in order to pursue unrelated political and ideological goals.

Unless there are more intensive attempts at racial mobilisation, we do not believe there will be a race war or anything approximating one in South Africa. Much of what passes for 'racial conflict' in South Africa is a cynical attempt by racial zealots to silence different opinions or deflect attention from sound and often well-intentioned criticism by crying 'racist' – a phenomenon that the professor of philosophy at UCT, David Benatar, describes as 'a recurring and noxious feature of human history'. South Africa's race relations remain good, which is remarkable considering our history, current weak economic performance, and the efforts of agitators to turn South Africans against each other. That race relations have been able to withstand such stresses shows just how much common goodwill there is among South Africans. One could go as far as to suggest that, considering what the outcomes might have been, race relations are one of South Africa's real successes. Yet there is no room for complacency. If current levels of economic underperformance continue, it will become easier and easier to damage those positive relations, and perceptions may then begin to turn across the colour line, with devastating repercussions for South Africa's future stability.

Chapter 6: The political race

While the politicians complain about what they see as active efforts to destabilise the country, they are too slow to concede that such efforts could only succeed where confidence in the credibility of political parties was already very low. That crisis of political credibility is best understood by examining the steep drop in popular support for the ANC. The ANC won 63% of all votes cast in the first national election of 1994. That figure peaked at 69% in 2004 before falling back to around 63% in 2014. At first glance it seems like a stable performance for a still popular party. Not necessarily. A far more important measure than the election result is to look at what percentage of South Africans over the age of 18 voted for the ANC in each election – in other words, of all the people who were entitled to vote, what percentage actually got out of bed on election day and went to vote for the ANC? On this measure the ANC's support has fallen from 54% in 1994 to just 36% in 2014. Some of the ANC's lost support went to the DA and some to the Economic Freedom Fighters (EFF). However, most of it has ended up in the category of non-voters. A non-voter is someone who is over the age of eighteen but chooses not to vote, and there are more people in that category than people who vote for the ANC. The fall-off in voter participation is not political apathy, as it has kept pace with the increase in protest action. The non-voters are still politically engaged, and this makes them the great unknown factor in South African politics. Consider that if just half of them vote again, and not for the ANC, then the ANC will lose its national majority. This could happen by 2019 – although 2024 is a more likely date.

If the ANC does lose its national majority, that does not have to be because any other party beat it outright. Rather, we may end up in a position where no political party has over 50% of the vote, in which case at least two parties will have to join forces in order to form a coalition government. The combinations could be ANC–DA, ANC–EFF or DA–EFF. Each of these is possible and each will fundamentally shift the trajectory of our country.

The EFF's potential kingmaker role in a coalition future brings us to the second great unknown factor in South Africa's politics: whether the EFF is an opposition party at all. We think it is not, rather describing it as an exiled franchise of the ANC, established under protest, and retaining much sympathy within the mother body. Run the numbers, and if the ANC wins 49% of the national vote, EFF numbers might well rise to around 15%, 16% or 17%. If those estimates are anywhere close to accurate, a national-level ANC defeat followed within days by an ANC–EFF coalition will see what will essentially be the 'new ANC' emerging more powerful than it was before its defeat. We know that this is the EFF's long-term strategy just as we know it to be the fall-back position of many ANC leaders should the now dreaded 'ANC – 49%' ever appear on the big screens at the IEC results centre.

The case for a coalition future became a lot stronger after the local government elections of 2016. Averaged across the country, ANC support levels slipped to just 54%. The DA took control of key cities by entering into a loose coalition of sorts with the EFF. Yet even in rural areas, support for the ANC showed a considerable degree of slippage. Whether or not those local elections are viewed as a realignment of South African politics depends on whether you believe the EFF to be an opposition party. Consider that in the 2011 local government polls (when the yet-unborn EFF was just a twinkle in its mother's eye) the ANC obtained approximately 62% of the local vote. That figure is now 54%, but add back the EFF's 8% and has anything actually changed?

The fact that the EFF is in some form of relationship with the DA should not mislead us about the true intentions of both parties. A trade unionist described that relationship best to us as a one-night stand. The EFF is using it to entrench its bargaining position with the ANC, and the DA needs to govern more cities, as its experience has been that where it governs, it grows stronger. Nor do we write off the prospects of a future DA–ANC coalition, believing there to be a long-term DA strategy to unite with the better sections of the ANC. There is a good chance that such negotiations are already under way.

Regardless of the permutations, running the country as a series of coalitions will be infinitely more complicated for the ANC than having carte blanche to make policy as it pleases. You would therefore expect a powerful incentive for ANC policy-makers to unite and arrest the economic slump that is eroding their political majority. This is especially so because of the near-perfect correlation that exists between confidence in the government and change in the real after-tax income of households – a correlation that senior ANC leaders are aware of. There can be no doubt that they understand the problem. Poll after poll has shown them that jobs are the thing young people want the most. They also know they can lose an election. Off the record this is freely admitted. Polls show that popular confidence in the future of South Africa has fallen from a high point of 73% in 2004 to just over 30% today – a collapse in confidence that few governments could survive. And yet South Africa's political Titanic, Africa's grandest liberation movement, does not turn from the iceberg dead ahead. Why?

Part of the answer comes from understanding how the government and the ANC are fractured. Essentially three factions exist.

The first group comprises the communists and the left. They emerged out of the trade union movement, the Communist Party, and various components of academia and civil society; their star rose in the aftermath of the political changes that took place at the ruling party conference in December 2007. They have sought to force an outdated and long-discredited form of ideological policy dogma onto the country. This is dogma that resents private enterprise, regards Western countries as outposts of colonial aggression, denounces 'CIA-inspired' plots to stir revolution, and prioritises state-led wealth redistribution over investment-led economic growth. It is their pursuit of ideology that created the economic circumstances that in turn set in motion the now-growing political opposition to the ANC.

The second group comprises the traditionalists. They come out of the more rural and ethnically homogeneous strongholds of the ruling party. Strong believers in the importance of traditional leadership structures, they regard Western forms of liberal democracy as an unnecessary and colonial extravagance. They are largely out of touch with the aspirations of younger South Africans. When an artist painted a portrait, later displayed in a prominent gallery, of the President in a strident Lenin pose but with his private parts exposed, this group was apoplectic in its rage at the disrespect displayed to the country's leader. This group is quite authoritarian, often frighteningly corrupt, and has little understanding of economics. In many respects they represent the bombastic 'big-man' style of politics that so many African countries have suffered through. It is a camp that exists purely to extract wealth out of the country, only occasionally looking up from the trough to growl at some journalist or pro-democracy activist. They are the parasitic elite, which exists at all levels of the government down to the smallest local authority, where the local political elite extract what wealth they can from what petty tenders they may issue.

For much of the period after 2007 these two camps have interacted fairly well and held the balance of power in the government. On a number of areas of policy, the communists have found it easy to take advantage of the policy and economic naivety, as well as the greed, of the traditionalists and have essentially duped them into endorsing policies that have done much harm to South Africa's economy.

However, as economic growth has declined and deficits have increased, together with rising popular dissatisfaction with the ruling party, the traditionalists seem to be losing confidence in the advice they have been receiving from their leftist comrades. The traditionalists do not hold firm ideological views. Their politics is about power and patronage. Protests and anti-government activism frighten them – and increasingly they blame the leftists for the economic crisis that now threatens their political mandate and therefore the fiefdoms of patronage they worked so hard to carve out. This is a most important development.

The leftists, worried at losing their political influence, do not have much room to manoeuvre. Some are quite afraid, unwilling to speak on the phone or send emails, as they suspect the police and intelligence people (who answer to the traditionalist camp) are watching and listening. In 2016 fearful rumours swept the trade and industry department that all the communists would be fired. Those on the left fear they have overplayed the political hand they were dealt in 2007 and, in creating the circumstances that have brought about a decline in support for the ANC, are now in a very vulnerable political position.

This presents an opportunity for the third faction of the ANC – the modernists. These include former hard-line ideologues who are becoming pragmatic and the more forward-thinking elements of the parasitic elite who are worried that the ANC may sooner rather than later lose control of the country. They are the *verligte* ANC that we described in the first book in this series. In a recent meeting a senior ANC leader remarked, 'We were all Marxists, but we are not sure that being Marxists is still the right thing.' These *verligtes* or reformists are neither liberal-democrats nor instinctive capitalists but have the pragmatism and ruthlessness to turn the policy environment around should they win the balance of power within the ANC. This modernist or reformist faction in the ANC is often overlooked in analyses of South Africa. Some argue that no such group exists, or that it has been swallowed up by the arrogance and corruption of the party generally.

If the modernist faction of the ruling party can form a new balance of power within the ANC, then a new range of reformist scenarios will be open to South Africa. Coinciding with a commodity comeback and stable global economic conditions, such a deal could conceivably secure the economic turnaround that the ruling party would need in order to head off what may otherwise be a future electoral defeat.

Privately, a number of senior ruling party and government officials will admit the economy is in crisis. They correctly diagnose the danger inherent in our high unemployment and low investment rates and accurately gauge the likely negative impact of ratings downgrades. Privately they even concede that the ANC will lose an election on current economic trends. But partly because of the three-way split in the ANC and the government, they have at times seem stuck, frozen in time, and unable to respond.

A second part of the reason why the ANC ship is not turning away from the iceberg is ideology. Deregulating the labour market, dumping destructive black empowerment policies, and giving investors certainty over their property rights are just an ideological leap too far and too emotionally draining. The best analogy to draw is that of a smoker. Most smokers will admit that smoking is bad for them. They have no argument with the medical science that it will make them very sick. They may even die a terrible death from smoking. It is expensive and unpleasant to those around them. People with their best interests at heart point all this out to them – and they agree. But they carry on smoking. The reason? They cannot stop. The addiction is hard-wired into them and they ultimately prefer to exacerbate the problem than adopt the solution.

There is also a third, and more sinister, reason why the ANC is headed for that iceberg. Where does all the ANC's trouble come from? White people tend to leave them alone – preferring simply to get on with their lives in peace and quiet. Afrikaners do their own thing. Business is only too eager to sign onto whatever empowerment edict is required. Foreign governments leave them alone. The rural poor are relatively docile. All the trouble the ANC faces comes from one place: the emerging or aspirant black middle class. These are the young leaders of the DA and the EFF, the activists, and the newspaper editors who battle to outdo each other in insulting the party's leaders on their front pages. These are the aspiring middle-class youths who led the fees protesters through the gates of Parliament and the marches to Luthuli House. They are the young people who make impassioned pleas for a new revolution, who scoff irreverently at the ANC's attempts to defend itself with stories of 'the struggle', and who taunt the ANC old guard for being irrelevant and out of touch. They are the Twitter and the social media generation who use those platforms to make fun of Jacob Zuma and his imperfect English. They are a new generation that represents the now-strong inverse correlation between levels of income and education and whether people support the ANC.

They so terrify the old guard that you have to ask the question: Is it really in the ANC's interests to fix schools or fund university students – or will such concessions simply swell the ranks of the opposition? If young black people are freed from lives of rural dependency, will they still back the ANC or will their ascent to the urban middle class empower them to push the ANC out of power altogether? Is it not safer then to keep them under the thumb of captured traditional leaders? Considering these questions, a former ANC strategist has conceded in private that the party might more easily survive a future of poverty and desperation than one of high economic growth and job creation.

What too few people understand is that maybe the ANC is headed for that iceberg to save itself. This may explain why more and more, since 2007, the drift of civil rights policy has been geared towards undermining those rights and eroding the property rights that anchor substantive human liberty in every free society. Examples stretch from South Africa's appalling voting record in the United Nations to attacks on the judiciary to proposals to regulate the media, political censorship at the public broadcaster, assaults on activists and civil rights groups, and at times brutal public-order policing. Some community activists tell frightening tales of assault and torture at the hands of the security forces. The Helen Suzman Foundation was raided by what appear to be rogue intelligence agents working for one of the ruling party's many factions – who made off with some of the foundation's computers. What is little known is that the police have established a counter-intelligence unit – the first since the apartheid era. Many municipal jurisdictions routinely deny applications for protest marches. There are examples of the government ignoring court orders. Some of South Africa's more prominent newspapers would probably not survive the withdrawal of government advertising. Much of the civil society community could be put out of business by proposed regulation of their funding sources. With one exception, the Chapter Nine institutions exist under the boot of the ANC and have been all but useless. The point is that South Africa's democracy is not nearly as resilient as many outside observers think, and much of it could be snuffed out quickly if the state was sufficiently motivated to do so.

All of this creates opportunities for the DA. The party has grown quickly from just more than 1% of the vote in 1994 to 25% of the vote today. It governs a province and a sufficient number of cities to substantiate the claim that it rules over more than 50% of South Africa's GDP. There can be no question about its commitment to democracy and civil rights. On the economy, it holds sound positions on the importance of growth, property rights, labour-market reform, and small business.

Because of this, you would think it could have gained deeper political traction than it has. One reason why that traction extends to just a quarter of voters may be that it is not the natural political counterbalance to the ANC. That role should always have been filled by the black consciousness movement, whose leader, Steve Biko, the apartheid government murdered, but whose ideas the ANC destroyed in its 'people's war' of the 1980s and 1990s. The white liberals escaped similar persecution, as the ANC feared this would turn European and American opinion against them and, by default, South Africa's main political alternative ended up being one that still seems somewhat alien to black voters.

Partly to address that problem, the DA has appointed a number of black spokespeople and leaders. However, the change in complexion remains insufficient to draw massive numbers of new supporters – particularly in a country where ordinary people are not nearly as race-obsessed as we are often told. What is far more important is the ability to offer a compelling alternative to voters – one that captures imaginations as a new and better way to meet unmet expectations. But on this score the DA has at times lost its way.

Take the example of a devastating column penned in 2016 by the

Business Day writer Gareth van Onselen, a former top DA thinker and strategist. Van Onselen writes of a radio interview in which Stephen Grootes of Radio 702 interviewed the DA's national spokesperson, Phumzile van Damme. Van Onselen transcribed the interview as follows:

SG: 'How would you say your policies are different from the African National Congress?'

PvD: 'Our policies are absolutely different from the ANC ...'

SG: 'But how are they different? I mean, give me an example.'

PvD: 'Ummm ... An example would be ... Uhhh ... I'm just trying to think of one quite quickly ...'

Grootes eventually prompts a response.

The point, which could not be more powerfully made, is that the DA seems unsure at times of what it stands for. For example, it was simply odd that the DA chose to endorse the National Development Plan – a half-baked wish list of policies written by its rival. Then in late 2016 the party set about a plan to introduce ANC-style racial quotas across all levels of the party from branch structures upwards – even as it opposed such quotas for national sports teams. Through adopting the same racial-ideological basis of policy as the ANC, the DA may in time come to backtrack on its commitment to property rights and market-driven economic growth. The risk for the DA is that as it pursues the plummeting ANC comet downwards, it is less than circumspect in appropriating for itself every policy and idea (and person) breaking off from the ANC. In time, in important areas of policy, it may then become difficult to distinguish the one from the other – possibly that is the intention – but it is a fatal mistake nonetheless, as the opposition will then have taken on board some of the very things that caused the ANC to plummet in the first place.

This problem is most acute in the hottest policy area of all – that of race, empowerment and redress. The DA seems trapped between either having to endorse the ANC's divisive approach to empowerment or being seen to reject the importance of redress entirely. It is a lose-lose outcome for the DA – either the party is 'ANC-lite' or it wants to bring back apartheid. The solution is straightforward: develop something new. What is needed is a fresh and compelling new approach to how South Africa can meet popular expectations and bring all its people into the mainstream economy and middle classes. This point is so important that the future of opposition politics hinges largely on the ability of the DA to develop that alternative.

Should it set out to do so, the party might draw some courage from the results of an opinion poll survey we conducted in 2015. We asked a representative sample of South Africans, 'Have BEE policies helped poor blacks?' The data in the table below sets out the answers; you will see that 58% of all South Africans and 60.3% of black people said that the policy had helped poor black people. This is undoubtedly the kind of result that deters the DA from moving too far from the ANC's position.

	Total	Black	Coloured	Indian	White
Yes	58.00%	60.30%	46.90%	63.50%	48.70%
No	41.90%	39.60%	53.10%	36.50%	51.00%

But we did not leave it there, probing deeper to ask: 'Have BEE policies helped your community?' An interesting thing started to happen as the answers changed. This time only 40% of all people and 44.2% of black people said yes – as you can see in the next table.

	Total	Black	Coloured	Indian	White
Yes	40%	44.20%	20.70%	23.70%	29.00%
No	59.70%	55.50%	79.30%	75.60%	70.50%

We then probed even deeper, asking: 'Have BEE deals helped you personally?' Now only 12.8% of South Africans said yes and just 14.2% of black people.

	Total	Black	Coloured	Indian	White
Yes	12.80%	14.20%	7.40%	5.50%	9.40%
No	86.30%	85.10%	91.90%	94.50%	88.60%

The real cracker of an answer came when the survey asked: 'Have you yourself been awarded a BEE tender?' The results in the table below were astounding.

	Total	Black	Coloured	Indian	White
Yes	10.50%	11.50%	5.30%	1.50%	10.00%
No	89.30%	88.30%	94.50%	98.50%	89.50%

Just 11.5% of black people said yes, but so too did 10% of white people. The data establishes beyond any doubt that the way the ANC practises empowerment is a fraud. Current empowerment policies cynically manipulate the historical injustices against black people in order to enrich a small elite – white as much as black. It is only in an abstract sense that South Africans support the idea of BEE and affirmative action as practised by the ANC. But in practice they do not know how or why this helps them – and how could they, as it creates neither jobs nor new businesses – the two things poor people say they want. This ineffectualness is a political gap that you could drive fleets of horses and carriages through, but the DA has failed to do so.

Matched with the shambles in the ANC, the inability of South Africa's opposition politicians to develop a compelling alternative set of policies for economic inclusion has allowed a political vacuum to develop, which is filled by the swashbuckling racism and Marxist economics of the EFF. The EFF proposes nationalising mines and banks and other private industry. The outcome would be that the state takes over the pension funds and investments of all South Africans, including the poor workers whom the EFF claims that it represents. Those workers would all end up working for the state. The state would own their homes and businesses, and have complete control over their lives – a cookie-cutter model of the dictatorships run by Muammar Gaddafi, Robert Mugabe, Fidel Castro and Hugo Chávez, all of whom destroyed their economies as a means of subjugating their people, and all of whom the EFF idolises. Essentially the EFF is promising to take black people back to the misery of apartheid. It is testimony to the common sense of young people that, despite their growing frustrations, the EFF has to date managed to obtain less than 10% of any vote. It should be a source of pain to the rest of the opposition that it achieved that much. The danger for the rest of the opposition is that the EFF learns from its relative electoral failures and drops the Marxist rhetoric in favour of something more pragmatic. There are some good thinkers in the EFF – and if they inject some economic sense into the party, it may one day play a prominent role in staging an economic turnaround.

For the time being, however, the ANC may continue to defile itself, the DA may continue to hesitate about whether to take the political gap, and the EFF may keep having a lark. As long as confidence in politics and politicians remains low, another type of organisation will continue to fill the void.

Non-government and non-party political groups such as trade unions, civil rights groups and community development organisations are becoming more prominent. The most prominent of these is AfriForum which, with over 150,000 paying members, is the de facto opposition in many small towns and often takes on the challenge of repairing the infrastructure and delivering other services that the state now fails to provide. Despite being much despised, it is a superbly effective organisation that does a lot of good. AfriForum's critics should be cautious in what they condemn, as the rise of the organisation heralds the emergence of many other community-based groups that take responsibility for the things the state no longer does effectively. These range from the provision of basic services to education to child care and security in small towns and large cities alike, right across the country.

As more communities turn away from the state, the latter will become more nasty and repressive. Freedom of speech and political association will be undermined – as the state tries to clamp down on groups that wish to escape its repressive grip. Social media will be the most important countervailing force to this trend, but research shows that bandwidth costs in South Africa remain very high by international standards while speeds remain very low. If this were to change, we predict a sharp upswing in social media usage, allowing young people to remain influential in shaping the intellectual climate in the country – regardless of what is screened on the state broadcaster's evening news bulletin. Improved social media access will also better allow people to organise efficiently into groups outside of the state that address concerns in their community.

The point is not to be too obsessed with formal political processes or too depressed at the detached state of the government and many of the politicians. If the state and the party-political establishment continue to let South Africans down, the trend towards community organisation, as pioneered by AfriForum and replicated on a smaller scale in towns and villages across the country, may offer South Africans a reasonable chance at a still somewhat successful future.

Chapter 7: Making order from chaos

We have in our possession a fairly rigorous overview of the living conditions, economic, social and political trends that are likely to combine to shape our future. But the sheer volume of information and the contradictory nature of much of it make for a chaotic and tangled mass of data and insights. We have seen, for example, that, contrary to popular perceptions, living standards have improved in South Africa yet protest levels and political instability have also escalated. We have seen that, contrary to perceptions, the ANC did well in increasing GDP growth and reducing debt and deficit levels when it came to power, yet it has exhausted all the easy economic levers that were open to it and South Africa now flirts with recession. There is a new middle class but approximately half of young people are jobless. Universities have performed admirably for much of the past two decades but schools have performed very badly. The universities are now at risk of following the schools downwards. Private sector healthcare services are world-class but hostile policy-making threatens that sector and the middle class it helps to retain.

As the middle class comes under pressure, the wealth redistribution that enabled living standards to improve seems ever less sustainable. Without much higher levels of economic growth, South Africa looks certain to destabilise further, but few government leaders are prepared to push for the reforms necessary for an economic recovery. On the contrary, despite South Africa's reputation as a bastion of liberty in Africa, many in the government are looking to undermine democratic institutions and property rights to force a stronger grip on power. Yet as politicians try to ramp up the power of the state, that same state seems increasingly less able to perform its basic functions – and people have started to move away into their own enclaves. Race relations remain sound, but a number of commentators and politicians are trying to foment conflict between races. Possibly, if economic conditions continue to worsen, they may succeed in turning South Africans against each other. The politics of the country seem to be evolving towards a new model where coalitions may run the country – except that we do not know if one of the major opposition parties is an opposition party. It may also be premature to talk of coalitions if the ANC's reformist camp gets its house in order. Yet even if that reformist movement were to prevail (out of the ANC or out of the coalitions), would global economic conditions ultimately undermine any sincere attempt at real economic reform?

Reflect on the paragraphs above and you realise we are no closer, unfortunately, to answering the question we set out to address of where this is all going to take South Africa by 2030 – if anything, we have only succeeded in further muddying the waters. A joke we tell many of the groups we work with is that if you are not confused about South Africa, then you have not been properly briefed. This is a point reached midway through many scenario projects. We have gathered and identified the information that will shape our futures but don't yet know how it will do so. To answer that question, we need to make order out of the chaos by untangling the information we have gathered. We have to take all the social, economic and political information gathered in chapters 3, 4, 5 and 6 and distil it into a manageable number of particularly influential trends and then envisage the extremes to which those trends could take us. We ran such an in-house exercise in the IRR in late 2016 and came up with over 40 major trends and their likely extremes:

The extent and reach of service delivery efforts, such as water and electricity rollout, have been impressive but the model upon which those successes were achieved has run out of steam. At the one extreme of this trend, we can envisage that highly effective service delivery may again occur (if the financing becomes available) and that rapid progress will again be made over a short period of time to improve the living standards of poor South Africans. At the other extreme, the living conditions of many South Africans will deteriorate as service delivery capacity is eroded, the money to finance it dries up, communities sit and wait for the state, and the state never delivers.

The welfare system has helped improve living standards and the consumer economy, but the money to finance that system is running out. We can envisage a future where an economic recovery ensures that the welfare system – which currently helps support the living standards of more than one in four South Africans – remains affordable and does much to sustain living standards. It may even be expanded if the economy grows fast enough. Alternatively, the real value of grants may slide as the welfare system collapses in the face of high inflation and a widening budget deficit.

The middle class has doubled in size. At one future extreme of that trend, we may reach the required economic growth rates and deliver the quality of schooling to double the size of the middle class every ten to fifteen years and in so doing develop South Africa into a middle-income society. On the other hand, stunted growth and assaults on democratic institutions may see much of the middle class emigrate while those that remain become an even smaller elite who live in enclaves surrounded by seas of relative poverty.

As expected, inequality levels have deepened – but this is more a political than a social or economic problem. We can see one future in which South Africa may grow at rates fast enough that middle-class expansion reduces inequality over a number of decades. Alternatively, it may become a more equal society through mass impoverishment – where everybody becomes equally poor.

South Africa's schools perform really badly and condemn more than half the country's children to a future of unemployment and welfare dependency. However, with sufficient reforms to education policy we may become a country where every child has a good chance of obtaining excellent schooling. We may also remain a country where only a small minority of children, possibly even a declining minority, attend good or adequate schools.

Tertiary education institutions have performed strongly to date and more institutions, especially technically focused ones, must be added to create new post-school education opportunities for young people. That could happen if the financing and institutional autonomy such institutions need are available, and South Africa could develop into an emerging market leader in post-school education. But the danger is that we head into a future where the quality of higher education institutions will quickly deteriorate, putting an end to South Africa's better-case scenarios.

South Africa has exhausted its surplus electricity capacity and much new coal/nuclear/gas capacity needs to be commissioned. With sufficient forward planning, management skills and financing, it is possible to imagine a country in which the new commissioning takes place and sufficient supply is guaranteed. However, without proper planning and sufficient finance we will enter a future of constant electricity interruptions and blackouts.

Alongside the question of future electricity supply is the question of a future water crisis. On the one hand, if the correct water policy and management decisions are taken, we see a future South Africa where the water demand of households and industry will be met. But where the wrong decisions are taken, a prolonged drought accompanied by deteriorating infrastructure may see erratic water supply and considerable human suffering.

Crime levels remain extremely high and the collective trauma inflicted is understated. Only in an environment of highly effective policing can we foresee crime rates declining to international norms. If such policing is not forthcoming, we see a South Africa in which communities will be increasingly forced to take law enforcement into their own hands to defend their lives and property.

South Africa has weak family structures, and this enables the violent and destructive behaviour of many young people. At one extreme of this trend, rising prosperity and social conservatism may see a future

South Africa in which family bonds strengthen. At the other extreme, those bonds will deteriorate further and a future South Africa will generate generation after generation of vulgar, violent and lawless young people.

Apart from the issue of family structures, too few young people play a positive and inclusive economic role in the economy. In a somewhat distant future we can still see how young people may become educated enough to be absorbed into the labour market where – as taxpayers and consumers – they help drive an economic recovery. It is considerably easier, unfortunately, to extrapolate a future in which young people are never absorbed into the mainstream economy, become a burden on limited resources, and contribute to accelerating South Africa's political and economic destabilisation.

Urbanisation has accelerated. This trend may continue and a future South Africa will then be a largely urban society. Alternatively, steps may be taken to halt the trend and place the greatest possible proportion of young people under the control of traditional leaders in rural areas.

Public healthcare resources are stretched, but the private sector provides cost-effective, world-class standards of care although government policy now threatens the private sector. At one extreme, South Africa's healthcare policy-makers may take decisions that bring us to a future where the professionalism of the private sector is increasingly applied to the public sector. On the other hand, South Africa will gravitate to become a society where the demands of the public sector are used to destroy the private sector.

The single most important trend of all relates to economic growth, which performed strongly in the middle to late 2000s but which is now moving towards possible recession. There is still enough substantiating evidence to propose a future where reformists, aided by global conditions, stage a recovery in which growth rates reach and maintain levels of around 5%. Yet there is also a future South Africa in which no substantive reforms are introduced and very low, even negative, rates of economic growth are experienced.

Per capita GDP rose quickly in the 2000s but then flattened out and is now declining. It is possible to imagine a future scenario in which per capita GDP again rises quickly. But on the basis of current trends, we will experience a future where GDP per capita will decline and may even go into free-fall, triggering a range of political consequences.

Interest rates were halved after 1994 but may have bottomed out. There is a plausible future in which rate hikes are moderated and rates later decline beyond present lows. However, it is also possible to envisage a future in which rates increase quickly as inflation runs away.

Related to interest rates is the question of inflation, which for much of the past twenty years has been maintained at levels of around 6%. Sensible economic policies may result in a future where the inflation trend is kept in check. However, reckless policy, such as accelerated printing of money or a sharp devaluation in the currency, may see inflation levels spike very quickly and even take South Africa into an era of hyper-inflation.

Bond yields have declined by half since 1994. If a measure of policy and economic certainty is maintained, we can imagine a trend where yields continue at around present levels. However, in the event of a series of credit downgrades and much new populist policy-making, a future will unfold in which yields will increase very quickly, undermining the government's ability to develop and maintain infrastructure.

Government debt was cut in half after 1994 but has been allowed to rebound to apartheid-era highs. On the one hand, it is possible to anticipate a future where debt levels are allowed to escalate as a share of GDP, meaning that the interest bill of the government will crowd out other areas of expenditure. Debt levels may accelerate to the extent that South Africa needs to approach the International Monetary Fund for a bailout. At the other extreme, there is a South African government that borrows cheaply and effectively while keeping its debt levels and interest bill in check.

The budget deficit was well managed after 1994 and in two years surpluses were even recorded, but deficit levels are again on the rise. At the more positive extreme, this trend will again reverse as a mix of future austerity measures and high economic growth keeps the deficit in check. At the more negative extreme, this trend will see the deficit blow out as a reckless future government spends wildly in a desperate bid to stay in power.

The current account deficit benefited from the commodity boom for much of the ANC's first two decades in power, even as consumer demand for imported goods increased. At one extreme, a resurgent industrial export economy, matched with a commodity comeback, takes us to a future where the deficit is kept in check even as consumer spending recovers. At the other extreme, deindustrialisation and a lack of domestic economic competitiveness could see exports dive and the deficit increase, even in the absence of increased consumer spending.

For much of the last twenty years the government practised sensible conservative economics, but in 2007 that changed and economic policy has become more ideological and populist. We can envisage a future return to economic common sense. Alternatively, we can envisage a South Africa that follows the lead of scores of failed socialist societies and adopts a deeply ideological approach to policy-making that wrecks the economy.

Property rights have generally been respected but are now under growing threat. A future reformist government that is serious about increasing living standards and positioning South Africa as a competitive emerging market may put an end to the threats and secure property rights. But there is undoubtedly also a potential future in which most property rights are ceded to the state.

South Africa had a very sound reputation as an investment destination until 2007, but that has now changed and foreign and domestic investors alike are looking at ways to reduce their exposure to the country. A future turn in policy may reverse that trend and South Africa may again become a highly desirable investment destination – this is still possible. Alternatively, the current trend of anti-investor hostility may accelerate to force investment capital out of the country.

South Africa shows low levels of established entrepreneurship, and yet future job creation will demand thousands of new small businesses. We can see one future in which enabling policy and legislation, together with a buoyant economy, sees thousands of young people start their own businesses. There is also a future in which a weak economy and a hostile government make it very difficult for small businesses to succeed.

South Africa has doubled the number of people with jobs even as the unemployment rate remained at uniquely high levels. Accelerated growth may see the unemployment rate fall and South Africa may become a country where the rate approximates emerging market norms. At the other extreme of the employment trend, however, a low-growth future may see mass job losses and a decline in the labour-market absorption rate.

Labour-market policy has been and remains hostile to job creation, with South Africa plumbing the bottom of global labour-market rankings. A future is possible in which the government amends labour-market policy to price poor people into work. Alternatively, a future is possible in which lawmakers continue to price poorer and less skilled workseekers out of the economy.

Trade unions have for the most part acted to deter investment and protect the employed from the unemployed. However, the trade union trend could change under new future leaders, and unions could play a constructive role in supporting new job creation. Alternatively, they could continue to play a destructive and obstructionist role and help take South Africa into a future where more jobs are lost and more investment leaves the country.

South Africa has lost a large number of skilled people to economies that offered them better prospects. This trend may be reversed if sensible migration and domestic economic policy decisions are taken. South Africa may even come to attract top foreign skills. On the other hand, it is not difficult to foresee a future where domestic skills continue to be pushed out and foreign skills denied entry.

Global economic trends exert a particular influence on South Africa's economy. At one extreme of that trend, a sustained global economic recovery greatly increases the likelihood of South Africa staging a domestic recovery. At the other extreme, a global crash will put paid to any short- or medium-term prospects of economic recovery in South Africa.

Technological innovations are coming to take the place of human workers. South Africa may become a future case study of this trend as companies seek to avoid the risks linked to hiring human workers. Alternatively, South Africa may find a means to employ such innovation not just to increase growth rates but also to improve labour-market absorption.

The top end of the commodity super-cycle was very important in helping to reach growth levels of 5%, and the commodity fall-off has hurt South Africa's export economy. That fall-off may reverse and higher global commodity prices may turn out to be an unexpected windfall for South African policy-makers. However, if commodity prices stay lower for longer, then South Africa will be forced to diversify its export economy if it is to have any chance of staging an economic recovery.

The structure of GDP has shifted over the past two decades to reflect a post-industrial economic make-up. It remains possible to argue that South Africa may stage a reindustrialisation comeback, which will see primary and secondary industries contribute a growing share of GDP. In the absence of such a comeback, the trend for the GDP structure will be one that sees a continued evolution in the direction of a high-skilled tertiary economy.

The government is generally incompetent and inept at putting policies into practice. However, it is conceivable that this may change and that if good policies are developed, they may be implemented. Alternatively, even if sound polices are developed the government may not have the management skills to put them into practice – in which case any move towards reform will be stillborn.

Confidence in politicians is waning and faith in the political system is declining. We can envisage a future in which that may change, politicians develop compelling policies, and a growing proportion of people turn out to vote. Alternatively, another future can be imagined in which people reject the formal political system as being irrelevant and look instead to localised home-grown systems of parallel government.

Violent protest levels are escalating and developing racial overtones. In one future, a combination of improving living standards and/or ruthless policing may reduce the number and intensity of protests. In another future, it is possible to envisage a national-scale uprising against the government.

Current trends show the ANC losing support. However, an economic recovery or the return of the EFF could see the ANC remain in power for some elections to come. Alternatively, its weakness could intensify and cause it to lose either the 2019 or the 2024 elections.

Ideology prevents many senior leaders in the ANC from seizing the solutions to its crisis of diminishing support. As in many socialist societies, this may change and the leadership of the party may become increasingly pragmatic. Alternatively, there is a future in which dogma dominates the policy decisions of the ruling party.

The opposition has grown in influence but has failed to fully exploit the weaknesses of the ANC. The trend of opposition politics may evolve to see a future opposition leadership present a compelling alternative set of policies to those of the ANC and winning (through coalition or otherwise) a national political majority as early as 2019. At the other end of the opposition trend, such parties may become progressively less relevant.

The state is increasingly intruding on economic and political life even as it becomes weaker. At one extreme, a future South African state may play a central and dominant role in determining the trajectory of the country – for better or worse. On the other hand, it may wither and decline as the role of individuals, smaller communities, businesses and other non-state actors comes to determine the future trajectory of South Africa.

Non-state and non-political actors such as civil society and community groups have become very influential. This may remain the case and these groups may in time become alternatives to the state. On the other hand, the role and influence of non-state actors may diminish.

As the government comes under pressure, it has engaged in dirty tricks to undermine the freedoms enshrined in the Constitution. This trend may be reversed under a future government and South Africa could remain a beacon of liberal democracy. Alternatively, the current trend may accelerate and free speech will be further curtailed, free political association discouraged, and activist and opposition groups actively persecuted.

Social media is important in shaping opinions. The free use of social media may both support the maintenance of democracy and serve as a platform for violent incitement to revolution. Because social media is such a potent agent for political change, it is heavily regulated in draconian societies, and this may be the route through which South Africa's social media trend will evolve.

Race relations are sound but an effort is being made to turn South Africans against each other. There is a future in which relations remain sound and even improve further as the economy recovers, but we can also anticipate a future in which race and ethnic groups turn on each other.

The trends identified here represent a rigorous collection of the forces that will shape the direction that a future South Africa could take. You can also see the extent to which that direction is rendered uncertain by the broad extremes to which each of the trends could potentially evolve. Notwithstanding those extremes, the list provides a more precise and ordered presentation than the broad sweeping analyses of South Africa that were offered in chapters 3 to 6. However, such a number of trends, no matter how neatly presented, remain an unwieldy mass of information from which to determine how the future may unfold.

To overcome this problem we seek to group the trends set out here into an even more manageable number of key driving forces. These are the collective, overarching and definitive trends around which our scenarios will be structured. Reducing them to a more manageable number does not mean that any of the detail or nuance is lost, since when the scenarios are written up in later chapters of this book those write-ups will incorporate how each of the trends set out here played itself out in every scenario.

When the challenge of grouping the trends was presented to IRR colleagues, the following key driving forces emerged:

The first key driving force is related to expectations about the future and whether these could be met. This driving force arose from many of the social trends around issues such as job creation, education, service delivery, housing and electricity access. At the one extreme, popular expectations would be met over the next decade. This would imply that the country had the resources to meet such expectations. Implicit in that assumption was a healthy economy, sound financial indicators, a buoyant private sector, massive new job creation, the establishment of thousands of new businesses and an effective government. On the other hand, expectations would not be met. In this outcome the economy would not create the fiscal and employment space to meet expectations. Job creation numbers would fall far short of demand. The government would be inept and inefficient, and people would be very unhappy and probably very angry.

A second key driving force is related to ideology. Here the one extreme would see South African policy-makers remain trapped in a dated, Soviet-inspired ideological worldview that would prevent them from freeing the economy to reach its full potential. The other extreme would see South African policy-makers learn from the experience of highly successful societies and economies, many of which had themselves thrown off the yoke of dated ideology, to introduce and implement bold new policies that would allow the country to reach its full potential.

The third key driving force is related to public opinion around questions of policy and ideology. Would ordinary people support sensible policy or rather follow the populist and ignorant views of radical but charismatic political leaders? If the public did not embrace the need for policy reform, then the prospects for a reformist government would be in doubt unless such a government had the unbridled power to force its edicts onto a sceptical society.

A fourth key driving force is related to the role of the state. South Africa could have an extremely dominant state that interfered in the minutiae of people's lives, dictated what they should think or do, and determined their living standards and quality of life. Alternatively, the role and influence of the state could decline and South Africans might start to look to themselves and their communities to improve their own lives. Non-state actors would then become more prominent.

A fifth key driving force is related to civil rights and freedoms. South Africa could remain a free and open society in which free speech and free political association were able to thrive in an unhindered manner. In such a future, political opposition parties could win elections, for example; alternatively, rights and freedoms might be eroded to a point where the Constitution becomes meaningless. In such a future the ruling party could cling to power through violence, fear and repression, even when expectations were not met.

A sixth key driving force is related to the global economy. South Africa is not an island unto itself and its long-term economic evolution will be intertwined with that of much of the rest of the world. A sustained global economic recovery could see South Africa follow other emerging markets and countries in Africa upwards. A long-term global slump would make a South African recovery so much more difficult and perhaps impossible.

The seventh key driving force is related to race and ethnic relations and societal cohesion. One extreme of this force would see South Africa remain a cohesive whole. The other would see extreme racial and ethnic tensions exacerbated by anti-establishment rhetoric, a scenario that could see South Africa fracture into politically, socially and economically isolated and distant communities.

These seven trends represent some progress in untangling the mass of data and information with which we started. Think of them as the distilled spirit of chapters 3, 4, 5 and 6. Each of the seven driving forces will have a definitive and primary impact on the type of country we become. To start building the scenario matrix, we need to rank these forces on the basis of their relative impact and uncertainty and then select the most impactful and uncertain trends as the axes of that matrix. This sorting for impact and uncertainty is done on a table with two axes. The vertical axis tracks relative uncertainty while the horizontal axis tracks relative importance. The graphic below shows how the final assessment looked.

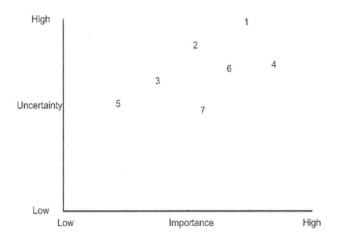

The most impactful and most important trends congregate near the top right quadrant of the graphic, and it is these that we use to build the scenario matrix. Our argument is that the capacity to meet popular expectations is the *most uncertain* trend facing South Africa. This will become the vertical axis of the scenario matrix. There is no guarantee that the political emancipation of the country will be followed by an economic one. Even from where my IRR colleagues sit, with decades of experience and the best possible information at hand, it remains too difficult to make a definite call that by 2030 South Africa will be meeting the expectations of the great majority of its people.

The trend of the *greatest impact* on how our country will evolve will be the role of the state, and this becomes the horizontal axis of the matrix. The state may play a dominant but positive role in driving reform and raising living standards. It may equally play a repressive role. It may also play an increasingly limited role, leaving it to people themselves and to non-state actors to take charge and drive South Africa towards the type of society it is destined to become.

It is possible to disagree with this assessment and see some other trend as more uncertain or more important. You may also feel that somewhere along the line we have missed a trend that will turn out to be important. None of that matters. The scenario method we are using is such that, as long as our initial analysis is sufficiently robust and most major trends were incorporated into our analysis, the scenarios that emerge will be similar, regardless of whether we choose slightly different axes for the matrix or trends with which to populate the later scenarios. If our initial analysis is broad and rigorous enough, then we will arrive at very similar scenarios each time, regardless of which specific axes we choose. The graphic below shows how the scenario matrix looks.

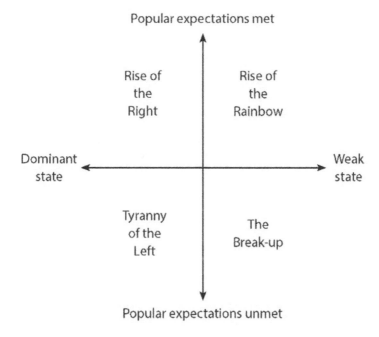

The four quadrants of the matrix represent four possible future South Africas based on how the most important and uncertain forces shaping the future play out over the next decade.

The top left quadrant describes a world in which the state plays a dominant role in the society and popular expectations of a better life have been met. For reasons that will become clear, we will call this scenario the *Rise of the Right*. The top right quadrant represents a South Africa in which the role and influence of the state are limited but popular expectations have been met. This one is called the *Rise of the Rainbow*. The bottom left quadrant represents a South Africa dominated by a powerful repressive state in which expectations are still unmet. We will call this the *Tyranny of the Left*. Bottom right is a South Africa in which the state has withered while popular expectations remain unmet. We call this *The Break-up* scenario.

Each of these is a possible country that may unfold over the next decade, and we may have the experience of living in any one of them. All the chaotic and contradictory information incorporated in our initial analysis of the condition of South Africa has brought us to the point where we now have a degree of direction about how the future will unfold. What must be done next is to develop a detailed description of exactly what life will be like in each of these worlds. To do this we will bring back into the analysis all the social, economic and political trends that have already been identified and predict how each one will evolve in each scenario. Think of these descriptions as reports, written from the future, that tell us how the country we live in has changed. In the final chapter we will make the case for which of the four we believe will materialise.

Chapter 8: Rise of the Right

It has been ten years since South Africans went to the polls in their 2019 national and provincial elections. Over the past decade tumultuous change has taken place in the country. South Africa is governed by an authoritarian state that has suppressed civil rights in order to force a very successful set of economic reforms onto the country. Constitutional rights and freedoms have been eroded but living standards are up. The economy is performing strongly. South Africa stands as the leading example of a new breed of authoritarian African capitalist economies.

For much of its first twenty years as a democracy, South Africa was seen as a free and open society with an underperforming economy. The political rights and freedoms won in the transition years of the 1990s had not been matched by sufficient improvements in the economic circumstances of South Africans. Nor, did the critics warn a decade ago, would economic freedom ever be attained. Events of the past decade have proved most critics wrong. South Africa has pioneered a new model of authoritarian capitalism that is starting to take root across the African continent. It is a model that has seen an erosion of democratic rights and freedoms. The state has been ruthless in the suppression of free speech and free political association. Protesters have been shot in the streets, journalists and opposition leaders have been exiled, jailed and, in the worst cases, assassinated. The civil rights culture that South Africa was thought to be pioneering is all but gone. The retreat of democracy has, however, been accompanied by a great improvement in the material conditions of almost all South Africans.

Drive across the country from large cities to small towns, and the extent to which basic living standards have improved is inescapable. The example of housing is perhaps the most striking: a highly effective, state-driven housing policy has delivered an extraordinary increase in the proportion of households living in a formal house. The data tells the story. In 1994 the proportion of households in a formal house stood at 64%. By 2010 that figure stood at just below 80%. Housing delivery numbers slowed in the years between 2010 and 2019 as the economy became sluggish and government revenues fell, but as economic growth picked up into the early 2020s the picture began to improve, and now more than nine in ten South African families live in a formal home. Most of the construction is taking place by means of state-subsidised construction companies. Continued rural-to-urban migration and declining average household size mean that approximately one in ten households still live in informal structures, but current housing trends suggest that this backlog will come close to being eradicated over the next twenty years.

The quality of the homes built over the past decade is also much improved compared with what was being built in South Africa's early years as a democracy. Housing budgets have increased and the state has become much more efficient in all that it undertakes. Corruption in the civil service has almost disappeared. You cannot buy your way onto housing waiting lists. Crooked officials who try to sell state-built housing are jailed when they are caught. Affirmative action and cadre deployment practices in the civil service have been done away with. The civil service is a meritocracy in which the elites of society are proud to serve; and in the housing department, as in all other government departments, ineptitude, laziness and corruption are not tolerated.

Improved housing delivery is just one measure of the improvement in overall living standards, which is true of almost all service delivery indicators. Nearly all households now have access to electricity, an improved water source and municipal refuse removal. In many cases delivery is taking place through state-subsidised utilities and parastatals. The reliability of such services is excellent and there is no comparison between the slack and corrupt state-owned enterprises of a decade ago and those of today. Technocrats and the best students of every university graduating class, not cadres, now run these entities.

Improved state-led service delivery efforts have been accompanied by a significant expansion in the reach of the social welfare system. Just a decade ago it appeared as if that system was running out of money. Real increases in grant levels were running at well below the effective inflation rate in poor households. That has changed, and increases in welfare grants have over recent years kept pace with inflation. This has helped to bolster household income levels, which have in turn supported overall increases in household expenditure. A food-stamp programme has been introduced, allowing poor households to buy state-subsidised staple foods (bread, milk, maize meal, cooking oil, and also products such as baby formula and nappies). A new basic income grant (or BIG) was introduced. There are also jobseeker grants as well as a programme of study grants for tertiary students.

The effects of improved service delivery and expanded welfare provision have been further strengthened by improvements in the quality of schooling. Aside from a handful of elite private schools, all other schools are state-run and the state dictates all curriculum content. English is the exclusive language of teaching and children are prevented from using their mother tongue on school grounds. No fees are paid and parents are prohibited from raising extra funds to develop new facilities or hire extra teachers. There is a moratorium in place on the issuing of licences to operate new private schools.

The quality of teaching and discipline in state schools has been greatly improved. Pass rates have been restored to respectable levels. State education authorities have little tolerance for poor discipline from either pupils or teachers. Strict uniform and behaviour standards are enforced. Authorities encourage corporal punishment – which is prevalent. The Department of Education has waged a successful campaign against teacher unions, which had been instrumental in provoking instability in the school system. Strikes and stayaways by teachers have been banned. Those who challenged the bans were prosecuted and lost their jobs. Authorities introduced a schools Inspectorate Division, which tours the country reviewing conditions and standards. Teachers and school principals fear the 'ID' inspectors, who arrive unannounced and have the power to bring charges and suspensions against teaching staff. Absenteeism by teachers is punished. School principals who fail to meet the required standards for academic achievement lose their jobs.

The effect of the changes in school policy can be seen in South Africa's matriculation results. The number of children passing Mathematics with good grades has tripled over the past decade. The same effect can be seen in South Africa moving up international rankings of school performance. Throughout the apartheid era, and for much of the first two decades after 1994, the life prospects of young South Africans were determined by the school they went to. Research suggested that almost 80% of public schools were badly managed and delivered very poor results – condemning the children who attended them to a life not much better than their parents had. Parents were desperate to get their children out of the state system and into expensive private schools. That has all changed. The education reforms have won much support from parents, who no longer have to pay fees and are able to send their children to the nearest state school secure in the knowledge that they will be well educated.

Improved school education has been matched by changes in the higher education sector. Universities have lost their autonomy and fall wholly under the control of the Minister of Education. Enrolment levels were cut to ensure that only the most capable students won places at university so that the limited places and funds were not wasted on weaker students. As in schools, the state has taken a very strong line on standards and discipline on campuses. Protest action and dissent are not tolerated. The police have been used to put down the few (now rare) attempted student uprisings. Rebellious student leaders are arrested and expelled. Student political organisations and several civil society groups have been banned from campuses. Only those groups approved by the minister are allowed to engage in student politics. A new financing model has been introduced whereby graduates pay increased levels of income tax, which is used to subsidise later generations of students.

While standards at universities have improved, an even greater reformation has taken place within technical and vocational colleges. These are producing the artisans that are building the next phase of South Africa's economic expansion as a resurgent industrial economy in Africa. The state has built scores of such campuses around the country and staffed them with the best technical and vocational instructors it could find – including teaching staff imported from abroad. The same rules that apply to university campuses also apply to these colleges. They answer to the state, college heads are appointed by the Minister of Education, the colleges are state-subsidised, high standards are maintained, and no student dissent or political activity (beyond that authorised by the minister) is permitted.

Most major port, rail, road and air travel infrastructure is built, maintained and managed in partnership with state-owned corporations. Much of that infrastructure is well beyond its sell-by date but is nonetheless kept in operation because demand is so high and the engineers that do the maintenance are sufficiently skilled. State planners, as well as the Eskom parastatal, have secured significant new investment in coal- and gas-fired electrical generation capacity. A new state-subsidised gas corporation is completing a gas pipeline that runs through southern Africa around the South African coastline to feed a new fleet of gas turbines. A series of new inland coal-fired stations is being financed and built by the state. New nuclear capacity is expected to come online over the next decade. South Africa is also importing significant amounts of energy out of southern Africa, where South African energy parastatals play an influential role in raising regional energy production levels. The energy sector is one of the fastest-growing economic sectors in the country.

Industrial and household demand for water increased very quickly as the economy expanded, urbanisation increased and living standards rose. Anticipating the onset of a water crisis, much of the state's infrastructure development focus of the past decade has been on water. Almost all that development is being undertaken in partnership with state-run development corporations working closely with municipal authorities. The improvement in water management relates not only to infrastructure. The quality of ground and surface water sources is being protected by water management authorities. Improved urban living standards, and the declining number of shack settlements, together with the professional management of municipal water services, have halted sewage dumping into watercourses. Strict environmental controls, which are enforced effectively by the Department of Environmental Affairs, prevent industrial contaminants from entering rivers, dams and groundwater. Violators face steep fines and may have their business licences revoked.

Just as South Africa has seen improvements in basic service delivery, education standards and public infrastructure, great progress has been made in the delivery of universally high-quality healthcare services. The 2019 cabinet took a number of firm decisions around healthcare provision. Private facilities were required to cede a 51% shareholding to the state. Graduating doctors and medical professionals are required to do service within the state sector. Private medical schemes were partly nationalised to finance expanded public sector healthcare provision. Policies of affirmative action and cadre deployment in the public healthcare sector were discontinued. Nursing unions were banned from operating within the grounds of hospitals or clinics. Strikes by healthcare workers were made illegal and strict new standards and levels of service delivery were enforced by the Health Minister. Despite being much criticised, these policy changes have had the effect of increasing the quality of care available from the public healthcare sector. Middle-class households are increasingly opting to receive certain healthcare services in the public sector. Improvements in public healthcare access have also benefited from the increase in the number of doctors and nurses graduating from South Africa's medical schools and new state-run nursing colleges.

Compared with where South Africa was a decade ago, this is a totally unanticipated reversal. A number of journalists and analysts have asked what led to it. How did an inept and ideologically incapacitated government turn to lead what is becoming one of the emerging world's most impressive success stories?

From all the answers that have been suggested, the most important is that the government and the ruling party were afraid of losing the lucrative networks of patronage and corruption they had worked so hard to carve out since 1994. The results of the 2016 local government elections showed that the ANC might lose a future election and, with it, control of the state. If that occurred, it would be cut off from the patronage networks that held that party together. If that happened the party would fragment and its supporters would desert it in even greater numbers. What was needed to prevent defeat was what party insiders called a new model of 'sustainable wealth extraction'. This would be a political system in which the South African economy grew fast enough to create the economic opportunities necessary to restore new popular confidence in the ANC at the same time as allowing the party and its leaders to extract massive amounts of wealth out of the tax base. The template that the ANC had in mind was that of the Asian Tiger economies, such as those of Singapore, South Korea and China. The party was also greatly inspired by the pioneering steps towards such a model in Africa under the rule of Hailemariam Desalegn in Ethiopia and Paul Kagame in Rwanda.

Shocked by the 2016 election results, reformists in the ANC staged what was effectively a right-wing coup within the party. This was a brutal fight and left scores of bodies in its wake as leftist ideologues, unionists and communists were leveraged and ground out of the movement. What remained was an authoritarian and undemocratic leadership – an alliance between the traditionalists and reformists – that now had a mutual interest in securing the economic expansion of South Africa. The result was a shift to the ideological right in the form of an increasingly authoritarian and anti-democratic political order that used that authority to force growth-focused economic policies onto the country.

Very few analysts or business leaders had this new political and economic model on their radars and were initially alarmed at the changes that took place within the party and the government. The ejection of leftist leaders and the growing prominence of securocrats frightened them. This was, after all, the corrupt side of the ANC that was gaining the upper hand in the party's internal power struggle. The cliché reformers such as Pravin Gordhan were being sidelined and isolated as the hardliners took over. In retrospect, if they had paid more attention to developments in other parts of the continent, most notably those in Ethiopia and Rwanda, they might have better understood what was actually taking place in South Africa.

The success of the reformist agenda rested on two operational pillars. The first was the professionalisation of the civil service and the second was the authoritarianism of the state. As the state was going to lead South Africa's economic turnaround, it needed to rely on a world-class civil service, hence the hard line that was taken against affirmative action and the deployment of inept cadres. Corruption by low-level civil servants was not tolerated and was punished in trials televised on state media – corruption was to become the sole preserve of the party elites. Ineptitude, laziness and rudeness to the public were cracked down upon just as harshly.

Authoritarianism was the second pillar, as the reforms were immediately unpopular and controversial. Labour unions and activists were outraged at changes to labour laws that abandoned minimum wages, reduced protections for striking workers, introduced strike ballots and removed the horizontal application of bargaining council agreements. Academics were outraged over the loss of independence of universities. The private sector was concerned about increased intervention in the economy and the forced seizure of private assets, as seen in the healthcare sector. The black business elite was alarmed at proposals to halt affirmative action and racial preferencing policies and return the economy and the civil service to a meritocracy.

As resistance to the reformist agenda grew, the state cracked down. This it had to do, since allowing the reforms to be stalled or delayed could well bring about the political demise of the ANC. Foreign-funded civil society groups were faced with new restrictions on their activities in South Africa. If they persisted in challenging the state, they were banned, their local leaders arrested and their foreign staff deported. Journalists were required to register with the newly established Department of Information and could lose their accreditation to report in South Africa if they fell foul of media laws. Those who ignored restrictions on reporting were detained by the police, and many complained of being assaulted in custody. A number left the country. Community protest leaders were arrested and intimidated by the police. Some reported being kidnapped and interrogated by nameless security agents, only to be released after a few days of interrogation. Opposition parties were subjected to new funding and campaign restrictions and fell victim to dirty tricks perpetrated by the intelligence services. The most prominent opposition leaders were detained on fabricated charges. Court orders were ignored and judges were bribed and intimidated while the state gained more control over judicial appointment processes. Business leaders who criticised the government saw their companies lose operating licences and permits.

Despite all the abuses that were perpetrated, the crackdown was effective in curtailing what might otherwise have been mass resistance to the reformist agenda. The number of anti-government protest actions has dwindled to almost zero over the past decade. There is a near complete absence of dissenting opinion in the mainstream media. Opposition politics has slumped into near-irrelevance.

For people who did not understand the country well, that this type of political system could have established itself at all seemed incongruous. South Africa was, after all, meant to be Mandela's rainbow nation, a beacon of democracy in a repressive world. But for all the imagery and pageantry it put on for the world, South Africa was always a deeply conservative society and that conservatism, a piece of common ground between black and white, is what has come to the fore in shaping modern South Africa.

The depth of the conservatism can be seen in how South Africans have welcomed the brutal policing tactics that accompanied the 2019 transition. Crime levels, and especially violent crime levels, have fallen sharply. South Africa's murder rate had fallen from approximately 67 murders committed for every 100,000 people in the country in 1994 to around 33 per 100,000 in 2014. The murder rate has now been cut to below 10 per 100,000 in 2029.

The post-2019 government saw law and order as a primary policy priority as disorder and anarchy might easily have been exploited to derail its reformist agenda. Restoring law and order could never be achieved through an inept and corrupt force. The police ministry therefore launched a drive to identify and fire corrupt officers. Respect for the chain of command was reinstalled. A professional officer corps was developed and deployed to run police stations and individual police units. Public complaints were taken seriously. As discipline returned to the force, levels of corruption and incompetence declined and popular confidence and trust in the police increased. The force became more professional, as seen in perfectly neat uniforms and professional interaction with the public. Corruption has been almost eradicated. As happened across the civil service, better management practices are delivering results. Increased resources have been invested in the justice system, and policy changes in regard to sentencing and young offender legislation have helped to cut levels of recidivism and deal effectively with the social causes of crime.

With a loyal and disciplined force in place, the state adopted a hard and uncompromising stance against violent and anti-social behaviour, especially among young people. Critics say that politicians gave carte blanche to the Police Commissioner to restore law and order in particularly violent communities. The number of criminal suspects killed by the police has grown exponentially. Rumours of 'death squads' and extrajudicial killings are rife. Activists argue that the police undermine civil rights and act in an inexcusably heavy-handed manner. The defence force, which has increasingly been employed within the country, has been singled out for particular criticism from rights groups. Lawmakers brush these complaints aside and the general public cheer the lawmakers all the way.

Because of the policing reforms, South Africa's armed robbery and housebreaking rates have hit record lows. Victim surveys show that South Africans are less likely to be a victim of crime than at any point in the past 30 years. The private security industry has even declined in size as South Africans become comfortable again with the idea of placing their security in the hands of the state's law-enforcement agencies.

But there is a lot more to explaining the stabilisation of South Africa than the intimidating tactics of the state. Life has improved, living standards are up and the joblessness rate continues to fall. The middle class is expanding. The critical breakthrough was when the ruling party understood that its future would largely be determined by the performance of the economy. Counterproductive policies that scared off investors, made life for entrepreneurs difficult and choked off job creation were killing the ANC. The crackdown on democracy could only take the party so far and would have to be accompanied by an economic turnaround to be sustainable in ensuring long-term ANC political dominance over South Africa. That economic turnaround now stands as the apex achievement of the party.

Just more than ten years ago, in the run-up to the 2019 election, South Africa was in deep economic trouble. Debt levels had doubled since 2008. Consumer confidence levels had reached the lowest level in decades. Mining and manufacturing production numbers were falling. The country was on the brink of recession, and there was nothing sustainable about the corrupt wealth-extraction model of the ANC. If the party's leaders continued to loot the fiscus, they would end up like ZANU-PF in Zimbabwe – bankrupt, dependent on foreign aid, and facing a popular uprising.

The right-wing coup that played out in the ANC received a welcome boost from global economic conditions that improved from the early 2020s. The United States led a resurgent global economy. South Africa's

European trade partners experienced sustained growth throughout much of the 2020s. Global commodity demand saw prices rebound as China grew into its excess infrastructure. India's continued strong growth helped support commodity prices. South Africa's burgeoning industrial base benefited from exports to growing urban consumer markets in Africa.

If economic events in South Africa from 2008 to 2018 could be described as a confluence of counterproductive ideological meddling in the economy and deteriorating global circumstances, the decade to 2029 represented the opposite. The state drove a highly effective economic reform agenda just as global economic conditions began to improve.

The best measure of the success achieved is that per capita GDP numbers grew strongly from 2019 on a trajectory akin to what South Africa experienced in the 1950s and 1960s. With growth rates now sustainably exceeding 6%, South Africa is looking to almost double its GDP every decade.

Higher growth and expanding household consumption, which remains the biggest component of GDP, have also been supported by interest rates, which have come down to levels well below 10%. Growing confidence in South Africa has also seen bond yields reduce, which has allowed the government the space it needs to borrow aggressively to finance its massive new infrastructure development projects. Increased government expenditure levels have coincided with declining government debt levels – a pattern that explained much of the economic success the ANC had achieved in the first fifteen years after 1994. Declining debt levels have reduced the government's interest bill, and the resultant savings have gone some way towards financing both continued state-led service delivery and welfare efforts as well as the increased investment in infrastructure.

Improved revenue generation has also allowed the government to keep its budget deficit in check even as it expanded the welfare programme, invested more in education and healthcare, and expanded domestic infrastructure. South Africa still runs a large deficit, but analysts are confident that the growth trajectory the country is on is sustainable and that the deficit is necessary to support the infrastructure expansion that is a key component of the growth story.

The current account deficit, which used to be one of the largest of any emerging market, has fallen sharply. The reasons for this include resurgent commodity prices as well as the export growth secured by South Africa's now-expanding industrial and manufacturing economies. The deficit has fallen despite the fact that the currency has strengthened for much of the past decade, while consumer demand for imports has grown with the increase in size of the middle class.

The success of the government's reforms has finally settled South Africa's 'battle of ideas' or the conflict over what ideological model should underpin South Africa's social and economic development. The model is one in which policy-making is centred within the ruling party. Decisions are made in the party by a small group of senior leaders in close consultation with trusted business leaders and economists. The party then instructs the government on what it should do, including maintaining a firm grip on sectors such as energy, strategic infrastructure, education and security while seeking to attract massive amounts of private investment into other economic sectors and rolling away all obstacles to such investment.

A compromise was reached around questions of property rights. The government 'gets it' that investors are not going to commit capital to long-term industrial expansion projects, precisely the type of investment South Africa needs, if there is no guarantee that they will see a return on that investment. Wild populist threats to nationalise everything from mines and banks to land for agriculture were dropped. However, the state has a right to free-carry (a free shareholding) in new investments across a host of economic sectors from banking to mining. All land is vested in the state, but secure 99-year leases have been made available to keep commercial producers on the land – something that has been a priority for the government. Water rights are vested in the state, as are rights to minerals.

In a marked reversal from a decade ago, the state goes to great lengths to attract private investment into industries that it sees as essential to South Africa's future economic development. Gone are the threats to 'destroy the capitalist system' that even cabinet ministers once made. The slurs that foreign investors are 'looting the country' (a description once used by a deputy minister) are fortunately no longer heard. The state has a rapacious appetite for new investment. Laws and policies that would deter or undermine such investment have been removed. Various incentives and subsidies are on offer, particularly to invest in poorer and more rural parts of South Africa. Anecdotal evidence is that the most senior party leaders skim a percentage off the top of most major new investments. Unlike a decade ago, however, this is not the type of corruption that is allowed to halt entire investment projects, bankrupt businesses, and turn into a looting free-for-all in which even the most junior government officials participated.

The economic recovery story is one that has seen South Africa break with its former dependence on commodity exports. The commodity slump that lasted from the mid-2010s to the early 2020s was a blessing in disguise for South African policy-makers. The reduction in exports and increase in the current account deficit that accompanied falling commodity prices forced policy-makers to accept the importance of supporting growth in a broader range of economic sectors. Manufacturing and agriculture have both seen their share of GDP improve and have helped South Africa to diversify its export base away from commodities.

Central to the successful attraction of more fixed investment in job-creating industries and poorer parts of the country is that most obstructive labour laws were removed. South Africa has seen its labour-market absorption rate increase by more than 10 percentage points over the past decade. Welfare is no longer the predominant source of income in many poor households but, rather, augments the income that young people earn through employment. Even as the welfare system has expanded, levels of welfare dependency have declined.

Young people are arguably the greatest beneficiaries of the government's labour-market reforms. Higher levels of absorption have served to mitigate their frustrations, which explains why young people are no longer seen as the destabilising force they once were. For many young people, easier access to the labour market has also served as an opportunity to obtain an education. The improvements in the quality of the state school system came too late for the young people already in the labour market. For that nearly lost generation, improved access to jobs has provided a second opportunity to learn new skills, which are helping them climb the earnings ladder. Research suggests that part of the decline in anti-social behaviour and crime rates among young people can be traced to their newfound economic inclusion as well as more stable family structures. Young people are seen not as a threat to stability but as a key factor in building a better future. They are the workers, business people, entrepreneurs and consumers who have turned South Africa into a leading emerging market.

This progress has been made possible not just through growth and labour-market deregulation but also through the far more productive and positive role played by trade unions in the country. Initially, in the first two decades after 1994, trade unions played in the main a destructive role in the economy. Seemingly, there was no understanding that in harming the economy job creation would fail, and unions would see their own influence decline. It was this very decline in union influence that allowed the ruling party to successfully challenge the unions on labour-market deregulation and to destroy those unions that got in its way. Public opinion in relation to unemployment was very skilfully used by the ANC to undermine more obstructive and militant union factions. What has remained of the union movement has now found common ground with the party.

South Africa's economic turnaround had the further benefit of reversing the net skills outflow that the country experienced after 1994. Young graduates want, and can now find, a future in the country. The government now offers incentive programmes for South Africans living abroad to return, and many families that left the country are returning. South Africa has also introduced immigration policies that seek to attract highly skilled people from around the world. This improved retention of domestic skills, matched with increased importation of foreign skills, has been an important pillar supporting the economic turnaround.

As much as the reversals in policy direction, what has drawn praise for the South African government is its ability to implement policies. There has been a shift away from drafting and talking about exceptionally detailed long-term plans only to redraft these and talk about them some more. Now the governance culture is one of action and ensuring that the foundations central to every stable and prosperous society are in place.

The effective implementation of sound policy has allowed South Africa to double the size of the middle class since 2019 – a phenomenon that is best measured in South Africa's bullish residential property market, where demand from young professionals has exceeded supply for much of the last four or five years. In 1994 the middle class was predominantly white. Within a decade the growth of a new black middle class was becoming apparent, mainly as a result of racial transformation in the civil service. As economic growth levels slowed over the difficult decade between approximately 2010 and 2019, growth in the middle class declined as employment growth slowed and rising interest rates and a weakening currency put mid-income households under great financial pressure.

But for the past decade middle-class growth has been back on the map. The difference for the immediate post-1994 era is that the civil service is no longer the prime incubator of the emerging black middle class. Children of black parents who found their first professional jobs in the civil service are entering the private sector as entrepreneurs. South Africa's demand for highly skilled professionals is rising much faster than available supply. This demand for skills, and the ease with which black professionals are playing a dominant role in the economy, have taken away much of the racial animosity that was festering between the black and white middle classes a decade ago. South Africa is a country that is creating significant new opportunities for skilled and hard-working young people, and the zero-sum game attitude that positioned black against white in a conflict over limited resources is no longer the prism though which South Africa makes economic policy. Instead, both black and white South Africans derive the mutual benefit that accrues from living and working in a high-growth economy. Another reason why racial tensions have dissipated is that South Africa has become a more equal society. This is not a question of absolute equality. Significant income and wealth gaps remain. However, across all class and race groups living standards are improving, and this collective improvement in the standards of living of all South Africans is promoting a new sense of common purpose and social cohesion. The state also does not tolerate racial agitation, for fear that such agitation might be employed as the nucleus of an anti-government protest movement.

Although South Africa is criticised often over the erosion of its civil rights culture, the country's economic success has been heralded across the emerging world. It is Africa's leading economy, and the model it helped to pioneer is set to transform the African continent into a prosperous and increasingly stable series of high-growth economies.

Chapter 9: The Tyranny of the Left

It has been a year since South Africans dejectedly went to the 2029 polls in what independent observers widely regard as a rigged set of elections. An all-powerful, and once popular, socialist government has destroyed South Africa's democracy. The economy continues its decline and no end appears in sight to the hell that South Africans have lived through over the past decade.

Fighting your way through the stench and expanse of litter that surrounds major urban areas and small towns, you cannot escape the growing impoverishment of South Africa. Streets are badly potholed and road markings have faded. Road signs are absent as urban decay sets in. The rural countryside reveals mile after mile of abandoned farms. The civil service displays the two worst attributes of African post-colonial administrations: cruelty and incompetence. Corruption is rife. South Africa shows all the signs of being the archetype of a failed post-colonial African state.

South Africans who return from abroad to visit say that what they notice most is that almost nothing new seems to have been built over the past decade, an observation that bears out the fact that since the fiscal crisis of the late 2010s the South African government has not had the resources to build on its former service delivery successes. Housing delivery, or rather its absence, is an example of the stagnation that has set in. Almost no new urban or rural housing delivery has occurred for the past decade, and shack settlements have sprawled amidst the decaying 'RDP' houses built ten or twenty years ago. So serious has the backlog become that the proportion of families in an informal house is again increasing, contrary to the trend in South Africa's first twenty years as a democracy.

Electricity and water delivery services are erratic. Regular power outages have become an inescapable part of life in urban South Africa – with the poorer urban peripheries being the worst affected. Water quality has declined as infrastructure cannot be maintained because the municipalities have neither the skills nor the budgets to do so. In many communities drinking water verges on being toxic and outbreaks of waterborne disease are common. Child deaths are regularly seen as a direct result of the infrastructural neglect by municipal authorities.

Living standards in poor communities were dealt a particularly crippling blow by the collapse of the government's once-expansive welfare programme. Grant payments, which once made up a significant source of the income of poor households, have become erratic. In many areas payments are not made for many months. Even when they do take place, in real terms the payments have fallen so far behind the rate of inflation that the value they contribute to many poor households is much less than it would have been ten years ago. A series of scandals has seen political leaders redirect money meant for grant payments into their own accounts. It is a pathetic sight to observe many people continuing to wait in desperation and demand that the government delivers on promises that now cannot possibly be met.

Research done by foreign development organisations reveals what is all too easy to see – that poverty measures have increased across the board. Child malnutrition rates have increased and a significant proportion of households cannot meet their basic food needs. Still-birth rates have increased. The proportion of the population living on less than US$2 per day, a number that was insignificant just a decade ago, is climbing year after year. Life expectancy is falling again as a new HIV and AIDS pandemic takes hold in a country that can no longer afford to finance a large-scale antiretroviral programme.

While the greatest hardship is experienced in poor communities, South Africa's middle classes have seen their living standards fall as the combination of a collapsing currency and hyper-inflation tore into their savings and pensions. Only those with significant foreign currency holdings or relations overseas have seen their living standards withstand the economic storms that have battered the country. Yet even this group struggles to repatriate funds in the face of a hostile government that tries to force them to convert foreign currency imports at official exchange rates into local currency units that have very little value.

The wealthiest of households have tried to take care of their own water and electricity provision through boreholes and solar systems and by bringing in private refuse removal providers, but nonsensical government regulations get in the way. Local authorities, for example, have blocked middle-class neighbourhoods from introducing private refuse removal services. The police service has banned neighbourhood watch schemes and the state has nationalised private security providers. State planners say they will not allow elitist neighbourhoods to flourish, calling them a racist attempt at undermining the government's service delivery efforts.

It comes as no surprise that emigration has seen the size of the white middle class fall sharply, especially in the younger age groups. Much of what remains of that class is at or nearing retirement age. There has also been a geographical shift in where that middle class resides – out of the northern parts of the country into the Western Cape, where they live in what remains of South Africa's mostly white middle-class neighbourhoods – trapped, essentially, in a country that resents them but from which they are unable to escape.

Not having the option to emigrate, the black middle class has seen its size diminish owing to declining real wage levels in the civil service as well as the fact that the economy has been in recession for much of the past decade and domestic business opportunities are limited. They are also trapped in a declining economy in which only the politically connected elite have been able to maintain some semblance of their earlier living standards. The country's politics is, however, so volatile that even for that elite consistently maintaining a middle-class lifestyle has become a trial – as different factions fall in and out of favour.

The irony is that while both middle classes are sinking, the black middle class continues to direct a stream of vitriol at the white middle class, blaming it for the mess the country is in. For the most part white people don't retaliate, simply putting up with the abuse and too afraid to say anything for fear that an argument could result in an even worse backlash. They grumble at their dinner parties and social gatherings about how the government has run the country into the ground, but these views are never expressed in public.

What knocked both middle classes equally was the government's persecution of the private healthcare sector. What was once merely populist anti-private sector rhetoric was translated into action, and the government introduced a series of draconian healthcare policies. Operating permits for many private medical practices were revoked. Private medical schemes were nationalised. People were forced to use badly resourced and poorly staffed national health insurance programmes. Doctors faced impossible new regulatory hurdles when it came to opening a practice, often being given the choice of setting up rural practices and charging fees set by the state or leaving the medical profession. Many private medical practices shut their doors, and more South African-trained doctors are thought to be working outside the country than within it. The logic was that in destroying the private sector people would start using public hospitals and the resources that once flowed into the private sector would become available to the public sector.

That policy failed so dismally that a handful of private clinics was allowed to keep their doors open to serve the political top brass and the elite of the middle class. But South Africa has lost its standing as an international healthcare leader and has even lost the ability to train high-quality doctors and nurses.

Deprivation and suffering are, of course, relative matters. In poor communities, the problems of healthcare access are very much worse than anything the middle classes have had to face. Hospitals are dirty and regularly run out of basic drugs. Waiting times can stretch for days on end. Water and electricity interruptions aggravate the already bad conditions. There are very few competent staff. Staff attitudes reflect the generally dilapidated state of the facilities they work in. So bad have conditions become that many South Africans seek to avoid the public healthcare sector and rather make do as best they can within their own communities. The public healthcare service has developed a reputation as a place where you go to die – more a mortuary and hospice service than a healthcare service.

What remains of the high-quality private healthcare sector, viewed against the appalling state of the public sector, is a useful prism through which to understand what life has become like in South Africa. The presence of the small and ageing white middle class and the small po-litically connected black middle class means that inequality levels have increased over the past decade (as the rest of society grew much poorer) and South Africa has secured its reputation as one of the world's most unequal societies. Less than 1% of South Africans are now thought to hold wealth equivalent to that of the other 99% – a good sound bite, but a number that arises from the effect of the collapsing currency on the offshore wealth of a tiny fragment of the society.

South Africa's economic decline owes much to the fact that educa-tion standards have collapsed at both school and university levels. A combination of shrinking revenues and bombastic state-driven inter-ference has destroyed what were once good public schools. Only the wealthiest South Africans can afford the foreign currency-quoted fees for South Africa's elite private schools where cabinet ministers rub shoul-ders with corrupt business people at sports days and prize-givings. Per-mits and licences have been denied to open lower-fee private schools on the grounds that these would take resources away from poorer schools, a move that halted efforts by middle-class parents to escape the poor quality on offer in government schools. Most families are forced to send their children to schools without books, libraries or laboratories, where teachers are idle and uninterested. The malaise in the school system can be seen in international benchmark studies that rank South Africa as having the worst Mathematics and Science results in the world.

As for university education, South Africans who can afford it now send their children to Europe and the United States. South Africa's once high-quality universities have crashed downwards through global rankings and very few retain international respect. The state has taken control of universities and forced curricula that teach mind-numbing Marxist doctrine to new generations of cadres and ruling-party apparatchiks. The standards are so low that many graduates can hardly string a series of coherent paragraphs together. The best academics have left for opportunities abroad. Comparisons are regularly made with the collapse of once-reasonable universities in many other African countries.

As living standards worsened and social tensions grew, so did crime levels. Police data is not seen as reliable but does show that South Africa's progress in reducing the murder rate, for example, in its first two decades as a democracy has been reversed. Using murder as a benchmark, South Africa now ranks as one of the world's most violent societies. There are high levels of street and violent crime. This is despite the police having become increasingly brutal – but many criminals are police officers or work in close co-operation with officers who have become a law unto themselves. The courts have become inefficient and unreliable. The forensic resources and prosecutors needed to secure convictions in criminal cases no longer exist. Most South Africans look for justice outside the justice system. Prisons represent terrible places of suffering comparable with the worst incarceration conditions anywhere in the world.

It is evident that the state sees the role of the police to counter pro-democracy activists and the courts as merely rubber stamps and institutions to keep corrupt political leaders out of jail. Beyond that, the state seems only too happy to allow individual police commanders a great degree of leeway to establish personal criminal fiefdoms. Indeed, if they did not allow this, the state would suffer the risk of a mutiny from within the poorly paid force.

The violent nature of the society is fuelled by family structures that have broken down even further. It is the breakdown of those structures that was arguably the most evil effect of the apartheid system. Now a similar level of breakdown is again occurring as poverty and desperation force poor households to send their most productive members to look for work far from home. Very few children are growing up with both parents in their household – a known predictor of anti-social behaviour. Match that with high levels of violence in poor communities and dysfunctional schools, and the position of young people in the country is dire.

Deteriorating social conditions are a reflection of the catastrophe that has played itself out in the economy. Whereas South Africa had recorded average growth rates in excess of 3% between 1994 and 2007, the growth picture turned sharply negative thereafter. Growth rates spent much of the decade after 2008 at levels of between 1% and 2%. The past decade has seen South Africa tip into recession as what can only be described as policies of state-engineered economic sabotage saw the country follow the earlier trajectories of once-promising emerging markets into negative growth territory.

Real per capita GDP levels have fallen consistently over the past decade and South Africans are now nearly 30% poorer in real terms than in 2020. The per capita GDP pattern matches very closely that of the 1980s, when economic uncertainty coalesced with a repressive government to reduce real GDP. The parallel with the 1980s is a good one, as in many respects South Africa today shows what would in all likelihood have happened to the country had the Vorster, Botha and De Klerk governments not shown a willingness to face up to economic realities and reform, but instead relied on the security forces and political repression to cling to power at all costs.

Stagnant and negative growth rates have corresponded with very high levels of inflation as the state pursued reckless policies and the real effective exchange rate weakened exponentially over a period of rising global oil prices. Inflation was driven further upwards by irrational increases in administered prices – such as electricity and water tariffs charged by a state desperate for revenues. Interest rates have been hiked in efforts to rein in inflation, but this has mainly had the effect of further undermining economic growth, consumer spending, the property market and the overall standing of the middle classes.

As the economic tide turned against South Africa, the country went through a series of ratings downgrades that put both its foreign and domestic debt at sub-investment grade. This triggered an outflow of investment capital as bond yields increased rapidly, which raised the cost of borrowing for the South African government. The budget deficit, which had been well managed between 1994 and 2007, was allowed to escalate as the government spent recklessly ahead of the 2019 and 2024 elections. Massive capital flight has taken hold and the joke is told that 'a South African and his money can no longer live in the same country'. Attempts at tightening exchange controls further hastened the outflow. There is almost no new foreign direct investment, and successful South African businesses are those that have diversified into Europe, Asia, America and the rest of Africa. It goes without saying that most of South Africa's top entrepreneurial talent has left the country.

The debt-to-GDP ratio escalated quickly as the government was forced to borrow increasing amounts of money in a bid to shore up expenditure on items such as social grants and civil service salaries, as well as bailouts for the growing number of state-run corporations, which are central to the ruling party's web of patronage. There has been a great expansion in the number of such state-owned companies in areas that range from pharmaceuticals to agriculture and mining. None of them generate profits, and they all consume large amounts of limited tax revenue. They are essentially conduits that launder money into the pockets of what the government describes as a new class of black industrialists.

Despite the turnaround in global commodity prices, South Africa's now firmly established trend of deindustrialisation means that it has failed to capitalise on its mineral resources to improve its trade balance. Declines in manufacturing and agricultural exports have contributed to a point where, despite reduced domestic consumer demand, South Africa's trade balance numbers are now among the worst in the world and represent a deficit with almost all its major trade partners, including those in Africa.

That the economic catastrophe has been orchestrated by state planners in pursuit of a long-discredited socialist ideology is widely accepted. But why, ask some observers, did the government of a country with such obvious potential adopt such a destructive set of policies?

The reason is that it was an effective strategy to keep the government in power in the same way that the same strategy has worked to keep dictatorial regimes in power in many other countries. The collapse of the education system, for example, was not simply a matter of neglect or insufficient resources. Much of the collapse was engineered by a government motivated by the fear of well-educated aspirant middle-class black people – or, as it once described them, 'clever blacks'.

Following the setback it suffered in the 2016 local government election, the ruling party came to identify a younger, better-educated and upwardly mobile class of black South Africans as the greatest threat it faced. This was the class from which the DA's new young leaders were emerging. It was the same class that was driving heightened levels of protest and anti-government activism, such as the student uprising of 2015 and the series of subsequent mass protests that ranged from the storming of Parliament and the Union Buildings to marches on the ANC's head office at Luthuli House. The badly educated, unemployed and welfare-dependent rural poor, many of whom live under the authority of tribal leaders, were regarded as a relatively docile class that posed no political threat to the ANC.

The party therefore saw the political advantage in choking off further growth of the urban black middle class, while slowing urbanisation and repatriating young people to rural areas where they would fall under the authority of traditional leaders. Party leaders delighted in the collapse of schools and the decline of universities – effectively allowing them to be burned by protesters. Housing delivery in urban areas was slowed. The authority of traditional leaders was expanded and they were bribed with higher salaries and fleets of new cars. Racial incitement and division were encouraged by the state in an effort to sow discord and prevent reconciliation across the colour line. The undermining of the private healthcare sector (but for the small fraction allowed to remain for the political elite) served the purpose of weakening the middle classes even further.

In the aftermath of the 2016 local elections, the ANC drew the laager tight around itself and set about choking off the black middle class while looking for scapegoats to blame for South Africa's accelerating decline. Statist and socialist leaders on the left of the party were emboldened to blame foreign investors and 'colonial aggression' for the 2016 results. Communists in the government called for South Africa to break its ties with Western democracies and global markets. The private sector was described as not having shared wealth, and calls were made for the state to play an increasingly direct role in the economy. White people were time and again blamed for the poverty, inequality and unemployment suffered by black people as the ANC sought to deflect scrutiny of its own failures into a divisive debate about race. In making South Africa's predominant national debate one about racial exploitation and colonialism, the ruling-party leaders were well positioned to argue that key economic sectors needed to be placed under direct state control if black South Africans were to be afforded a chance to share in the wealth of the country.

Scores of commentators, journalists, think tanks and civil society groups fell for the ruse. On university campuses calls were as extraordinary as that of 'Kill all whites'. Newspapers, even the business press, devoted many inches of column space to arguments about 'whiteness'. Conferences and lectures were called on how to defeat racism and often turned into festivals of racial hatred. The same became true of events ranging from book fairs to television debates. When black people joined opposition political parties, they were described as 'race traitors'. When they presented arguments about fighting corruption and the importance of growing the economy, they were accused of fronting for whites – as if corruption only harmed white people and only they would benefit from more jobs. Any dissenting voice was accused of racism. Even anti-apartheid struggle veterans and leading advocates against racial discrimination and injustice were accused of getting in the way of 'the revolution'. The courts were soon infected with such racial agitation and even the Constitutional Court started delivering judgments that were based more on prejudice than law. Rather than uniting to face down a violent, corrupt and incompetent state, South Africans allowed that state to turn them against each other.

The racial hysteria that swept the country was all the cover the ruling party needed to secure its survival. Destructive racial empowerment policies were ratcheted up, allowing a small coterie of politically connected business leaders to extort stakes in private companies. Companies that could not meet now draconian transformation targets were denied operating licences. Others were sent directives to surrender management and equity stakes or face forced closure. Labour regulations were further tightened as South Africa's export competitiveness dived. Usurping the independence of the universities was done in the name of liberating black students from oppression. The undermining of media independence was carried out in the name of racial transformation. The state's intrusion into more and more areas of the private lives of its citizens was motivated by the need for 'radical economic transformation'. The small band of reformist leaders in the ANC were effectively marginalised as the traditionalist and socialist factions got together to engineer a populist strategy that would keep the ruling party in power.

Central to that strategy was the destruction of property rights. The party regarded people who were able to accumulate their own wealth and property as a threat to the state. In denying them the right to own property, they could more easily be politically subjugated – particularly if they could at the same time be placed under the authority of traditional leaders. In appropriating the ability to seize property without compensation, the state positioned itself to punish what it saw as oppositionist voices and businesses. The strategy worked to secure the loyalty of a small class of party-supporting oligarchs whose prosperity could be tied directly to support for the party.

Initial populist appeals to undermine property rights played heavily into the historical land dispossession suffered by black people. This resonated with the maelstrom of racial agitation and anti-minority rhetoric that has become louder and louder over the past fifteen years. Through cynically manipulating historical land injustices, the state has perpetrated countless acts of seizure of private property without compensation. Such seizures started with land itself – the best tracts of which went to senior party leaders and the balance of which now rests under the control of traditional leaders in what has amounted to an expansion of the apartheid-era homelands policy. Very little land ever made its way into the hands of the poor peasant classes – the purported beneficiaries of the government's land seizures. Black landowners were disenfranchised even faster than whites. A few large industrial farming operations survived through corrupt empowerment deals with political leaders, but, overall, food production levels have fallen and South Africa is now a substantial net food importer – a position that, when viewed against the weakening rand, has greatly worsened the living standards of poor households.

The land seizures were a precursor to the seizure of other assets such as businesses and even movable goods, which were looted. If land seizures were a political mechanism aimed at the political subjugation of black South Africans, then the business seizures were an economic mechanism aimed at self-enrichment. Black Economic Empowerment ownership and management targets were ratcheted up to over 51%. Many smaller businesses folded while larger enterprises sold out and left the country – all examples that could be used as evidence of how 'white monopoly capital' and 'Western imperialists' were sabotaging the economy.

The self-enrichment of the political elite was, of course, a short-lived exercise as the government's rabid anti-business rhetoric, statist economic plans and seizure of private property had a chilling effect on the country's reputation as an investment destination. More often than not, such enrichment was simply a case of asset stripping – selling off the assets of newly obtained businesses and pocketing the cash or sending it offshore.

Declining investment levels triggered a jobs crisis, which further exacerbated the living standards crisis. The labour-market absorption rate declined to even deeper lows than fifteen years previously when South Africa already demonstrated arguably the worst absorption rate of any serious emerging market. While there has been employment growth in the state and the growing stable of state-run companies, real wage levels have fallen, payments to civil servants are erratic, and the state employment service is filled with corruption and ghost employees.

The jobs crisis was worsened by the draconian labour-market restrictions introduced after 2019. New minimum wage laws saw hundreds of thousands of people lose jobs as businesses shut down. Laws against temporary and atypical employment were enforced, which impacted most negatively on the employment prospects of relatively poor and unskilled people.

As part of its populist mandate, the now plainly Marxist state encouraged militant trade union action, which further soured the investment climate. Large corporations in industries from financial services to tourism were targeted for hostile union action, prolonged strikes and business shutdowns. Despite the damage that was being suffered, state planners hoped that the undermining of key economic sectors would create new opportunities for their personal self-enrichment.

The consequences, as experienced by ordinary people who lost their jobs, homes and pensions, were skilfully exploited time and again to demonstrate the extent to which the state had to be granted even greater powers before the poor majority of South Africans could be freed from capitalist exploitation.

So serious has been the damage done to the economy by the state that global circumstances hardly come into the equation when explaining South Africa's weak economic performance. Policy-makers had so geared South Africa to failure that even in the most positive of global contexts the country could not but have underperformed. The fact that global conditions did improve and that commodity markets came back quite strongly over the past decade is something that has largely passed South

Africa by. Even had the global economy settled into a prolonged era of low growth, South Africa would have remained largely unaffected by it all. The evidence for this can be seen in the fact that even though commodity prices picked up in the early 2020s, the state had done such damage to the mining economy and to the sentiments of the global mining industry that South Africa's mining exports have fallen despite the commodity price recovery.

Misguided policy and an insistence on centrally directed state planning also account for declining energy production capacity, which on its own might have been sufficient to forestall any chance of an industrial-led economic recovery. Private sector investment in energy has been forbidden and the once-promising public–private partnership model of infrastructure expansion generally has been jettisoned. Cabinet ministers are quite blatant in expressing the view that it is better to suffer from energy shortages than to surrender South Africa's energy sovereignty to private sector operators.

Partly because of South Africa's persistent energy shortages, the structure of GDP has continued to favour the relatively high-tech and high-skilled sectors. Yet even these high-tech services industries have looked to exit the country as the economy contracted. Those with broader African operations set up headquarters in other African countries.

The manufacturing economy has performed even worse. Despite the state's adoption of considerable protectionist measures, including import curbs, South Africa has failed to create competitive export-focused manufacturing businesses. Constraints on the labour market and union hostility, together with a declining domestic consumer market, have seen many manufacturing producers close their doors. Some were taken over through corrupt empowerment deals as part of a government programme to create a new class of black industrialists, but rising input costs, erratic electricity supply and unproductive labour have seen most of these enterprises grind to a halt. In many cases the subsidies provided to start new businesses were simply stolen. Attempts at rescuing these firms through state-driven recapitalisation schemes, which sought to turn them into new state-owned companies, have proved wasteful and ineffective and sacrificed precious and shrinking government revenues.

What has been particularly frightening about the past decade is the efficiency with which the government undermined the economy and the democratic order as well as the enthusiasm with which many South Africans initially encouraged the government. Business leaders had long complained that the government had good policies but just needed to learn to implement them. Their assessment of government policy has proved to be wrong and their wish for more effective implementation has become a curse from which the economy cannot escape. Regrettably, it is now true that whereas the state did not have the willpower to build a successful industrial economy, it has proved to possess more than sufficient willpower and determination to destroy one.

It seems incongruous when looking back that so many newspapers, academics and civil society activists initially welcomed the socialist inflection of government policy after 2008. They encouraged the state every step of the way to deepen its interference in the private sector, adopt ideologically driven reforms in the areas of labour, education and healthcare, and undermine property rights – the very moves that have allowed it such extraordinary power over individual South Africans. The destruction of the economic infrastructure was always merely a precursor to the assault on the democratic infrastructure. When the mood changed as people realised they were getting poorer, and public sentiment began to turn against the state, it proved too late and South Africans were trapped under the near absolute authority of the same politicians to whom they had willingly granted so much power.

In many post-colonial African societies, the most dangerous point in their political evolution came the moment the first post-liberation government realised it could lose power. For a time, the ANC's crude racial propaganda appeared as if it might work to keep the party in power, but despite the rabid nature of such incitement it was not enough to stave off growing resentment by poor and middle-income people alike, who saw their living standards decline.

To the horror of the ANC, over time the racial denunciations turned into denunciations of the ANC. Activists and the media accused the ANC of itself having sold out to 'white capital' and foreign interests. It was 'protecting business interests' and refusing to 'redistribute wealth'. The complaint seemed to be that what was being taken from the private sector and middle-class people had not been nationalised for the good of the people but was being divided among a small number of ANC leaders.

A new anti-ANC movement was gaining traction on university campuses and within foreign-funded civil society groups and was receiving a great degree of media sympathy. Street protests were becoming more common. Marches to ANC offices were arranged. Fearing the rise of a protest movement, the ANC set about introducing restrictions on protest actions. Permission to stage protest marches was denied. Activist leaders were arrested and some reported being tortured. Legislation was introduced to place civil society groups under state control. Intelligence and police agencies raided journalists' homes and newspaper offices.

These initial intrusions against civil liberties and free speech did not appear to have the desired effect and, despite increasingly extreme appeals to racial nationalist propaganda, the ruling party saw its local and national support levels fall further. By the time of the 2024 national election it seemed very likely that the ruling party could be voted out of office. Some news media and social media coverage of that era reveals the sense of naive euphoria that political change for the better was coming to South Africa. Socialist activists predicted the ANC would be voted out of office and its most corrupt leaders exiled, thereby ushering in the new era of a utopian people's democracy. More conservative analysts predicted the rise of a new era of reformist ANC leaders who, while not being democrats, would at least return some common sense and economic logic to the party and possibly secure an economic turnaround for South Africa.

Both the socialists' and conservatives' naively upbeat assessments, not to mention predictions that the ANC could lose an election, have proved to be very wrong. Anticipating its own defeat, the party moved swiftly and efficiently to dismantle South Africa's democratic infrastructure.

Opposition political parties became the focus of intense smear campaigns and intimidation orchestrated by the police and intelligence services. Opposition leaders were arrested and held in custody on trumped-up corruption charges. Often the state used such charges to show how serious it was about fighting corruption. In Parliament new rules were published to weaken the opposition, cut their funding and ban opposition lawmakers from access to certain information or taking part in certain debates. Harsh new non-profit organisation regulations were published that allowed the state to take over the affairs of any group that was deemed to be acting against South Africa's national interests. Many groups were taken over and later liquidated. New non-profit activist groups were denied registration. Foreign-funded groups were banned from operating in the country and their foreign staff deported. Draconian media regulations saw journalists requiring state-issued licences in order to work, and strict new censorship guidelines were introduced. Newspapers and news websites that broke censorship laws were shut down. When prominent editors complained, they were detained incommunicado and not even their lawyers could establish where they were. Even social media platforms were undermined and search engine results censored.

But despite the use of terror tactics to subvert opposition to ANC rule, the party continued to weaken. Not even its control of the Independent Electoral Commission seemed to be enough to prevent it losing its national majority. At the very moment that it appeared as though the ANC was at its weakest, and the South African nightmare might end, the EFF played its long-awaited political trump card and returned triumphantly to the ANC. This had long been the EFF strategy, and the party's leaders had simply waited for the moment at which the ANC would beg them, and offer any concession, to return to the party. In retrospect, they were never an opposition party but rather a front that had always retained a high degree of respect within the ANC. In splitting the opposition vote, the EFF created the illusion that the opposition was becoming stronger than it actually was. Just as the ANC appeared to be facing a national defeat, the EFF returned to the party to form a government with a constitutional majority. The new coalition completed the destruction of the democracy that the ANC had started, using their constitutional majority to put paid to many of the rights and freedoms that had until then been assured under South Africa's Constitution. The EFF leaders proved only too eager to return to the corruption and patronage networks that had hitherto been denied to them outside the ANC.

Initially these betrayals were met with popular outrage. South Africans turned to the streets and a series of massive anti-government protests followed – suggesting to some writers that a popular uprising against the government might succeed. However, these protests were met with brute force and a reign of terror. Protesters were arrested by the hundreds and scores of people were shot in the streets. Cabinet members spoke of the need for order and cynically demanded that protesters use democratic channels to 'air their grievances'. Protest leaders were charged with crimes and tortured in police custody. A witch-hunt was launched against those seen as fomenting protest against the state, and it saw thousands of arrests of journalists, academics, students, business people and activists, and the introduction of new security and 'anti-terror' legislation.

With the state having unleashed terror onto the populace and near absolute repression taking hold, South Africa is settling into a new status quo. Cowed communities have resigned themselves to their fate – accepting that they have been checkmated by the two political parties in which they had collectively invested so much faith. As the fear deepens, and with most avenues of political expression closed off, it is difficult to see how the now-dictatorial state might ever be dislodged. It would take a massive public uprising, verging on insurrection, to dislodge the state, but there is no sign of the public support, political organisation or leadership that such an uprising would require.

Chapter 10: The Break-up of South Africa

One year after the chaotic 2029 elections, South Africa has fractured, perhaps irreparably, along race, class and ethnic lines. The state is severely weakened and the economy has stagnated. Many South Africans remain very poor. Without any effective political leadership the country has become a society divided against itself. Against the odds, some small bands have built enclaves in which they maintain a largely normal life.

The best description of South Africa today is that of an enclave society. Drive through the big urban areas and you see the decay of the city centres, the unkempt roads and verges, the poverty of the sprawling shack settlements, the desperate people begging for work, and then, rising like a castle out of the squalor, the walls of the enclaves. The same thing can be seen driving down the southern coastline, where electrified security fences, floodlights and guard houses mark where 'South Africa' stops and the world of the largely autonomous golf estate or 'eco-estate' enclave begins. In deep rural South Africa, the countryside is interrupted by similar, stockade-like fences that mark where South Africa's last remaining commercial farmers have taken a stand against the collapse of the society around them.

There are two South Africas now: the one within the walls and the one outside those walls. They have very little to do with each other. Outside the walls the trends of gradually improving living standards that South Africa experienced between 1994 and 2008 have been reversed. As the economy wound down, the government ran out of the money it needed to provide housing, water and electricity services. Despite bold promises, there has been almost no state-led housing delivery for the past decade, as funds are diverted through corruption and new projects are not completed. The proportion of households living in shacks is again increasing.

The condition of South Africa's fields of previously built RDP houses is deteriorating as no upkeep or maintenance takes place.

The same tragic story plays itself out in relation to water and electricity delivery. Many of South Africa's municipal authorities no longer have the skills, budgets or capacity to deliver clean water services. The electricity grid and national power-generation capacity have fallen into disrepair. Supply is erratic. The proportion of households with access to clean water is in decline, and families are forced to make use of natural water sources such as rivers, dams and streams, even where these are often polluted and pose health dangers – reflected in increases in cases of diarrhoea amongst children.

Poorer households are being forced to turn to wood fires and coal stoves for cooking and heating while candles supply lighting. Fires regularly ravage the sprawl of shack settlements around South Africa's urban centres. As if humour could repel the awful reality, the joke is told, 'What did South Africans have before candles?' The answer? 'Electricity.'

Social welfare grants, which once played such an important part in raising the living standards of poor households, have seen their real value decline. Yet in the absence of employment growth and with little evidence of new entrepreneurial activity, many communities have simply accepted the decline in their living standards and South Africa has become a visibly poorer society. This impression is supported by data from international aid organisations and development experts, who report increasing levels of child malnutrition, disease and poverty in South Africa's poorer communities. Despite rising poverty rates South Africans seem unable to do anything, politically or economically, to help themselves out of trouble. The helplessness of it all is brought into stark relief by the presence of branded vehicles of the United Nations and other global aid agencies – previously an impossible sight in what should have remained Africa's most advanced economy. Western-backed aid agencies are stepping up their efforts at developmental support, including the provision of food aid, especially in poor rural backwaters where no productive economic activity is taking place.

As the agencies moved in, much of South Africa's educated middle class were moving out. Many young and well-educated South Africans saw little sense in sticking around in a society mired in corruption and incompetence. They wanted to live in societies that offered exciting career opportunities and good prospects for their children, and where the lights stayed on and water always came out of the taps. For many of them, South Africa remains a great holiday destination. They visit to show their children their home country and to spend time with their ageing parents, but it is not a society in which to live or make a life.

None of the social and economic decline has been malicious on the part of the state. It was not an attempt to undermine the growth of the middle class that once threatened the ANC's political hegemony – or anything of that sort. There is a far simpler explanation: South Africa has not had a government for the past decade, in the sense of an entity with a majority mandate and the ability to run the country. Rather, it has been in the hands of a series of confused, unstable and incompetent coalitions, none of which has had policy frameworks that, if implemented effectively, could have turned the country around. The result is that the state has weakened to a point approaching insignificance and South Africans have gone off in various directions to fend for themselves. Cynics say that the government governs over little more than the Union Buildings – but even there the once-impressive gardens are not what they were.

The chaos in government had its origins in the 2016 local government elections in which ANC support levels fell to a low of 54% and presented the possibility of the party losing its national majority in a future election. The first warning signs of the political fragmentation and confusion that now define South Africa soon followed. Rather than addressing the reasons for their declining support, ANC leaders turned inwards and fought with each other. Rather than seeking ways out of the morass, they sought to target scapegoats to blame for their weak performance. Fissures between the leftists, traditionalists and modernists in the party rapidly deepened. Soon a self-destructive all-out conflict raged from the corridors of Luthuli House to the smallest branches of the party. Party leaders and supporters broke into factions, which probably did more damage to each other than was done to the collective ANC by the efforts of the opposition. This was not a conflict of ideas but rather a fight over power, patronage and looting opportunities within the remnants of the economy. The fighting often turned to violence, and party insiders estimate that several hundred ANC members and several office-bearers have been killed over the past fifteen years.

The contagion of infighting also infected opposition politics. The ANC's near-defeat in 2016 had brought opposition parties together in what was hoped would become a new model of coalition politics for South Africa. However, the seduction of power and lure of patronage that came with governing proved too much of a temptation for smaller coalition partners. Corruption and power abuses soon began to manifest in the new coalitions. The DA sought to maintain some order within the coalitions, but this simply drew the ire of their new partners who variously denounced the DA, tried to sabotage its service delivery efforts and threatened to jump ship and go back to the ANC. By the time of the 2019 elections the coalitions had disintegrated.

The DA too, as the largest of the opposition parties, has had its own problems. Ironically these came from its growth. In growing as quickly as it did, it began to attract more former ANC voters and office-bearers – and was less than circumspect in whom it appointed to senior positions in the party. Yet many of these new leaders had left the ANC because of its corruption and incompetence – not because they supported the pro-growth and pro-property rights policies of the DA. They joined the DA because they saw it as the least corrupt and most efficient vehicle through which to pursue ANC ideology. This inevitably led to conflict around questions of race, redress and the role of the state, the outcome of which was that the DA suffered from the same internal instability that ensnared the ANC – although never to the point of bloodletting.

Opposition fragmentation and the break-up of the 2016 coalitions allowed the ANC to win the 2019 national election on a ticket of racial incitement and resurgent nationalism. However, internal squabbling and counterproductive ideological dogma saw the party fail to achieve the economic reformation that was necessary to meet the expectations of its supporters. The years from 2019 to 2024 saw the maintenance of low economic growth rates and no real job creation. Social welfare budgets came under greater pressure and protest levels escalated to new highs. Even when opinion polls began to show the likelihood that the ANC would face a national defeat in 2024, nothing was done by party leaders to avert that outcome and the ANC lost its national majority in 2024 and failed to achieve such a majority in 2029.

The ANC refused to enter into a coalition with the DA and fell out time and again with the EFF over who should lead a possible coalition. Smaller players had too little support for the ANC to cobble together a rag-tag national majority. For much of the past decade there has been no effective government and for the past five years no real government at all, as parties have squabbled in Parliament and at times refused to pass budgets or even agree on who should be President, much less agree on the reforms necessary to turn the economy around.

Activist groups led and organised protests and demanded change. Some business leaders took out advertisements in newspapers calling for change. The media called for reform and unity. Civil society groups brought lawsuits against errant ministers. But these efforts were largely ignored by the government. South Africans took to the streets to protest but the politicians just ignored that too. Without political guidance the police seemed unsure about how to intervene and protesters were left free to trash the streets. The media was not interfered with – even when it criticised the politicians. It appeared that the political leadership of the country had given up caring – perhaps realising that the protesters and critics were unlikely to change anything.

Initially the protests suggested a more united and inclusive country – black and white students protested arm in arm against university fee increases, for example. For a brief moment in time, there was the promise that South Africa's people might unite and force positive change even if its government and the politicians could not. Those hopes soon faded. It took little incitement for the protests to develop a nasty character. At first there were isolated racial and ethnic incidents, with scuffles and insults, which later became more commonplace. The absence of any effective law enforcement saw protests turn into riots. Black immigrants became targets of public rage, and xenophobic riots occurred with growing regularity across the country. All the while there were populist politicians and reckless journalists to fan the flames. The police remained ineffective and when they did intervene, their efforts further inflamed tensions.

When the politicians intervened, it was through crude racial nationalist incitement. Every flaw and fault in the society was ascribed to race, every failure explained by racism. Unemployment was the consequence of white business refusing to transform. Poverty was explained by the dominance of 'white monopoly capital'. Schooling was bad because 'the whites' hogged all the resources. Public healthcare was in a poor state because of the 'white-owned' private healthcare sector. The ANC had failed because it had 'sold out to the whites'. The DA would fail because 'there were too many white men in its leadership'. Even as it came in for racist criticism, the DA itself fell into the trap of ascribing South Africa's problems to race.

However, for all the noise, nothing changed. The protests and calls for change achieved nothing concrete, descending rather into factionalism and conflict within the protest movement itself while leaving the economy worse off than before, with the social fabric of the country bruised and battered. Nothing was done to address the actual problems facing the society – problems of low growth, bad schools and too few jobs.

Central to those problems remains the underperformance of the economy, which cannot create the wealth and employment necessary to meet popular expectations for improving living standards. Despite a range of weakening economic and business indicators, from manufacturing and mining production to consumer confidence, together with a number of business confidence measures, South African policy-makers have appeared to be paralysed in their inability to mount a coherent response to the growing economic crisis. This was as true when the ANC still held a national political majority as it is now after years of unstable coalition government. Where plans were written, no implementation ever took place. Despite appeals for economic growth and job creation, no action was taken to secure such outcomes. At times the government seemed to be merely a spectator of the economic collapse, and with no clear idea of what to do, it usually did nothing at all.

Instead of coherent reformist action, South Africa's politicians have displayed ideologically driven economic confusion and conflict – not just between political parties but even within them. In some quarters of the government there are ministers and officials who argue that South Africa needs more investment and economic growth. In other government quarters there are officials who contradict this and state that the priority of all policy must be redistribution. Even within departments confusion reigns. As one example, some officials within the Home Affairs Department are working to restrict skilled migration while others make proposals about how to attract more skilled migrants to the country.

It is not only that there are wildly contradictory strands of policy. Even when a policy is adopted there can be no certainty about how different officials, even those within the same government office, may enforce it. South Africa's remaining mining investors, for example, say that some mining officials interpret the rules around mining permits and licences differently from others. Every time these contradictions arise they lead to long delays and the costs are carried by investors. Government departments that are supposedly working together will often end up paralysing each other's efforts. The example of mining is again a good one to use: here, conflict between environmental regulators, the Department of Energy and the Mineral Resources Minister have created a Kafkaesque labyrinth for lawyers and mining advisers to navigate.

Such labyrinths are breeding grounds for corruption, which is occurring on a significant scale. Estimates suggest that a substantial portion of South Africa's GDP is being squirrelled away by corrupt officials, who use the impossible complexity of government policy together with inconsistent enforcement to carve out various dens of patronage.

Property rights, which are probably the most important area of policy, have been mired in uncertainty for years. Legislation has been passed that appears to allow the state to seize property largely by edict. However, confusion reigns because clear guidelines do not exist for how this should happen and the processes for seizure and compensation are in dispute.

In practice, the question of property rights has become a lottery. Seizures have been overturned by the courts in some instances but not in others. The risk of expropriation also depends largely on which faction is governing the corner of the country where your assets are located, or under which government department your business falls. The risk is also influenced by the perceived value to be looted from the specific property. A pattern is also emerging where one political faction unseats another and then expropriates its assets out of vengeance.

Hyper-uncertainty, combined with a government that has lost control of a large part of the society, means that there is not much to be said for South Africa's reputation as an investment destination. Studies show that neighbouring countries and the rest of Africa are attracting far more foreign investment on a per capita basis than South Africa is. A portion of that investment was previously domiciled in South Africa but was forced out due to policy confusion and the weak state of the economy.

A good analogy to draw is that South African lawmakers have spent the last several years on a slowly sinking ship. They knew the ship was sinking and they knew why it was sinking, but the sum total of their efforts to save it amounted to quarrelling with each other or seeking to instigate conflict among the passengers.

The effect of this lack of coherent economic action from lawmakers can be read in real GDP per capita numbers, which have been slowly falling for the last decade. As South Africans gradually became poorer and political tensions rose, this seemed to create even more intransigence on the part of policy-makers. Racial agitation took the place of making and implementing better polices. Analysts who predicted that declining economic performance would spark an economic reformation have proved to be very wrong.

As growth levels fell and interest rates and inflation rose, South Africa entered a long-term stagflationary stage in which the onshore wealth of richer people as well as the incomes of poorer South Africans were gradually eroded. The exception was those who had exported their wealth into foreign currencies and could now draw on this income to sustain their living standards and retirement. While South Africa has not fallen into a deep recession and pushed its budget over the fiscal cliff, its growth rates are far from sufficient to meet demands for jobs and expanded social services. The economy merely muddles along at a pedestrian pace that lags far behind the country's economic potential.

As uncertainty around South Africa rose, and the government appeared unable to act against the economic decline, a number of ratings downgrades took place, greatly increasing the government's borrowing costs. Together with the slow stagnation in tax revenues, this precluded any possibility of funding the infrastructure maintenance and expansion that would be a necessary component of any economic recovery strategy.

South Africa's only hope of financing such a recovery rests either on bailouts from international financing and development organisations or on renewed private sector investment. However, the various coalition partners in government are unwilling to accept the conditions that would be attached to such loans and still carry too much ideological resistance to drawing on the skills and money of private investors. There is very little prospect, even at this dire juncture, that South Africa's political leadership will be able to unite around a strategy for economic reform, and the current crisis is thus expected to deepen.

In struggling to attract investment, South Africa's past decade has been a jobs catastrophe. The youth unemployment rate increased. The theory, popular some years ago, that rising youth unemployment would prompt more subsistence economic activity and low-end entrepreneurship has proved to be incorrect. Quite the opposite seems to have happened and, driving around the streets of major urban centres, one is struck by the large number of idle and languishing youths.

None of this presents an economic environment that could have been expected to retain existing skills – not with high levels of economic growth across much of the rest of Africa and in the context of a global economic recovery. There were, of course, political and government leaders who saw the dangers of such a skills loss and sought to overcome them. But as has become the rule in South Africa, what one political faction or government department does is very quickly undermined and contradicted by another.

While the global economy has extracted skills out of South Africa, it has not done the same for exports. South Africa's export industries of mining, farming and manufacturing have performed badly as the government undermined them and as uncertainty about South Africa's political future grew. Miners can no longer reliably get their minerals to ports due to breakdowns in the state rail agency. Manufacturing exporters have seen their output levels decline as electricity supply became increasingly erratic. Despite a stagnant consumer expenditure environment, massive currency weakening (while not helping to drive exports upwards) has increased the costs of products, from fuel to food, that South Africa is forced to import.

The structure of GDP has come to be further dominated by high-tech and services industries such as finance, banking and information technology. This is not because these industries have been growing – the opposite is true – but because the primary and secondary industries have shown such considerable decline in their output levels. Former industrial parks at ports and on the urban fringes now stand partly vacant.

South Africa's schools were starved of funds as government revenues declined, and without any effective management their standards fell. Teachers' salaries are mostly, but no longer always, paid on time. Books and learning materials are often not available. Schools themselves are physically deteriorating. South Africa's education standards rank very low down on the list of African countries. Children graduating from the school system are often barely literate and generally unemployable.

The universities have also been allowed to decay and their standards now meet few international benchmarks. Enrolments, teaching and graduations still take place, but this has become to a large extent an exercise in going through the motions. There is little substance to what is learned or taught and degrees are often not worth the paper they are printed on.

The quality of public healthcare has similarly declined. Hospitals run out of drugs. Critical equipment has broken down and not been repaired. Staff are rude and inefficient. There are too few doctors and nurses available in the public sector. The country no longer has the capacity to train excellent doctors, and estimates suggest that the majority of South African-trained doctors and medical specialists now reside outside the country. Where foreign development agencies do not intervene in the healthcare sector, little is done.

The disappointment is that even the shared experience of declining living standards was unable to unite South Africans in a common new struggle for a better future. Economic tensions lent more momentum to deepening divisions that, together with a now almost entirely ineffective state, have seen the middle classes retreat into enclaves.

Some of the enclaves are effectively segregated along racial lines while others are completely multiracial microcosms of what South Africa's rainbow nation might have been. Regardless of their racial and cultural make-up, they all have in common communities that were forced to break with the state and take responsibility for their own affairs and welfare. These are communities that understand that the state has lost control of the country. They accept that the government will never provide for them and that South Africa will not return to normality for a considerable time.

As the state has weakened, and political parties have failed to find a way out of the morass, civil society and community groups became increasingly important. In the middle-class enclaves they play a more influential role in service delivery, education, security and economic development than the government does. In their separate ways, these groups have emerged to become parallel governments in the communities they serve.

Maintaining a largely normal middle-class life in South Africa requires taking control of, and responsibility for, water and electricity services, security and policing, schools and post-school education in the community in which one lives. The expansive urban residential estates and coastal eco-estates and golf estates follow this model, and residents pay a premium for the privilege of living there. The model works equally well in more middle-income neighbourhoods and small towns where community members are well organised and committed to making their town or community as successful, safe and comfortable as possible. It is a Plan B that works, and central to its success is a mindset shift from state dependency to extreme self-reliance.

Behind the walls of the enclaves, and in towns and communities that have accepted the need to become self-reliant, life can be good. There are excellent private schools and some very good tertiary institutions. In the more upmarket enclaves top-quality healthcare services are provided, together with shopping malls and entertainment complexes, offices, golf courses and sports facilities. Residents could in practice live their whole lives within the enclave and almost never have to go out. The latest developments even have their own solar-power systems and water-purification plants. Security is very strict, armed guards patrol the secured perimeters, and crime is almost unknown. The politicians may complain about the elitism of it all, but most members of the cabinet now reside in precisely such communities.

The effect is the creation of de facto independent communities that are insulated against the worst effects of the societal decay, violence and chaos around them. Once criticised as a throwback to apartheid, it is a model that the black middle classes have bought into as well. The ability of a community to go out on its own and take charge of its own affairs has become the distinguishing fault line between the more and less prosperous parts of South Africa.

Networks of the largest of the enclaves are approaching the status of independent city-states. Measured in GDP terms, they would compete on a per capita wealth basis with some of the world's richest societies. Self-sufficient in almost every respect, they are quasi-private countries that offer their residents the services, living standards and security that the South African government can no longer provide.

The fear of violent crime is important in understanding the fragmentation that has taken place in society. Shutting one's community off from the rest of society behind high walls has become the only effective strategy to prevent becoming a victim of South Africa's high crime rates.

The enclave phenomenon has spread beyond the middle classes and into very poor urban communities, where an emerging gang culture has taken advantage of the vacuum created by the weakening of the state. Violent gangs maraud in those communities and the state seems unable, even fearful, to challenge the authority these gangs have. In the absence of an effective government, they have become the de facto government in South Africa's urban slums, which might otherwise have descended into a state of anarchy.

Gang numbers have been swelled by the stream of unemployed and poorly educated young people – another lost generation and illustration partly of the consequences of the breakdown in family structures. Warnings about the political and social dangers of a lost generation of young people had been posted by analysts over much of the last twenty years. The government was specifically warned that the youth unemployment rate, which twenty years into democracy was in excess of 50%, was a recipe for political destabilisation. Policy-makers in the government failed to respond. The loss of authority that parents have over their children has helped fuel the lawlessness in society, which is an inevitable consequence of a society that includes so many unemployable young people who feel they have nothing to lose.

Race and class are not the only societal fissures, as ethnic divisions have also deepened. In a society breaking up along race lines, it did not take long for growing conflict over resources within black communities to assume an ethnic dimension. For years there had been undercurrents suggesting that some ethnic groups were favoured over others for tenders, jobs and government posts. As early as the mid-1990s there had been talk of an emerging Xhosa Nostra that monopolised opportunities for themselves. Part of the reason tensions have deepened is the resurgent Zulu nationalism that emerged from the changing power balances in the ANC. The ominous '100% Zulu boy' T-shirt worn by supporters of the Zuma-aligned factions of the ANC was a harbinger of what was to come. So, too, was the rejection by many ANC supporters outside KwaZulu-Natal of the idea that 'a Zulu' could govern over them. These tensions have erupted at times into conflict.

Traditional leaders were quick to capitalise on ethnic tensions. As national and provincial government structures weakened, these leaders became the de facto government in South Africa's poorer rural areas. Here they act as petty dictators. They demand taxes from businesses that operate in areas under their control. They discourage people of the 'wrong ethnicity' from residing in their communities. They dispense justice, control local schools and clinics, and assign plots of land for farming. They are well on their way to making rural South Africa regress to a system of ethnically segregated homelands. The more dire predictions warn of a return to the extreme levels of ethnic conflict that gripped South Africa in the 1980s.

As the unravelling of South Africa gains momentum, the idea of the future secession of parts of the country from the whole is discussed in social media and at dinner parties. An 'independence party' is active in the Western Cape. Some KwaZulu-Natal fringe politicians speak of breaking away from South Africa. But it is in many respects an academic debate – in practice the break-up of South Africa has already happened and it is unclear whether the society will ever be put back together again.

Chapter 11: Rise of the Rainbow

The elections of 2029 have delivered another endorsement for the now decade-old ANC–DA coalition. Economic growth rates have recovered and living standards are rising. Radical and destructive populist politicians have been isolated and South Africans are united in building a free and prosperous country.

Despite the fears of a decade ago, the ideal of South Africa as a rainbow nation has survived to thrive. Tour the urban peripheries as well as small towns right across South Africa, and you can see the progress that continues to be made. Compared with the squalor and poverty of a decade ago, South Africa is a country on the move. Every street is a hive of entrepreneurial activity. Rising prosperity has translated into a residential building boom as homes are being expanded. Particularly in poorer suburbs, this is a very different type of service delivery from what the country saw in its first decades of democracy, when the state had been the leading provider of housing in poor communities. Now it is people and communities that are doing it for themselves.

Three things have brought about the change. The first is that as economic growth and employment levels improved, so did the disposable income of households, which has allowed them to finance their own home expansion plans. The second is that government housing policy has changed. No longer is the state responsible for providing houses to people. It now provides title to serviced stands and has introduced financing programmes that allow households to qualify for bond-financing programmes, which are topped up with their own earned income, allowing families to commission their own homes from a wide range of accredited small-scale housing providers. The third change is the most important. The nature of the society has changed. South Africa is no longer a country in which people wait for the government to do something for them. It is one in which they will do it for themselves, and the government is there to help create the conditions for them to do so.

This is the opposite of the society of fifteen or twenty years ago when a dominant state was expected to lead economic and social development initiatives. At the time, a former housing minister complained that an old man had asked when the government would come to fix his broken door. She was horrified and questioned what type of society South Africa was building.

The growing sense of community responsibility and control over service delivery, in conjunction with support from government, explains improvements across a range of other indicators. Access to clean water sources is almost universal, while 99%+ of households now have access to electricity. South Africans will not accept anything less. If a small-town mayor or political party cannot deliver, they are quickly voted out of power. Different parties now govern different municipalities, and the competition this has engendered has secured a wholesale change in attitudes towards political accountability.

In terms of both water and electricity provision, local authority governments can no longer afford extended outages or erratic supply. It is no more the case that inept cadres are elevated to positions that they are manifestly unqualified to occupy. Most municipalities outsource water and electricity services to private providers according to competitive, cost-effective, transparent and therefore corruption-free bid processes. If the provider cannot deliver the service, they are quickly removed and replaced.

As the proven effectiveness of this model of service delivery established itself, the state came to delegate the responsibility for the physical delivery of services and focused instead on creating a competitive environment in which the best and most qualified service providers did the job. This change in policy had the added benefit of supporting the emergence of significant numbers of new entrepreneurs and small business owners.

As regards electrical generation capacity, some of this is still in the hands of the state, but in a context of limited resources and expertise and, most importantly, insufficient supply of electricity, the government took the firm decision to throw the electricity market open to competition. Almost all new capacity that enters the grid is privately provided according to contracts that are subject to open, accountable and competitive bid processes. The result is that South Africa now has the energy capacity to meet the increased demand flowing from an expanding economy.

The outsourcing of key services matched with much higher levels of economic growth has made possible the expansion of the welfare grants system. This programme is run very differently in comparison with a decade previously. Now poorer households qualify for grants that can be used to finance their own housing development, as already explained, as well as education and healthcare needs. These grants are paid in the form of vouchers loaded onto smartphones and cards that beneficiaries can use to access services at the point of sale. In addition, grant levels are higher for people who can prove that they are employed, engaged in entrepreneurial activity, or enrolled in government work schemes.

The voucher approach has done much to increase the decision-making power of households over how the grants they receive are spent. This has in turn helped to secure the accountability of political and government leaders downwards into communities. It is no longer a case that people are told by the state to attend a certain school or get their names on a specific housing waiting list. Households have the power to decide when, where and how they want to build homes, where to enrol their children in school, and how and where to access healthcare services.

As much as the welfare system has expanded, research into household incomes shows that grants now form a smaller proportion of such income, as households' earned income, from employment and entrepreneurship, is increasing at a faster rate than grant income. As the government removed impediments from the labour market and obstacles to entrepreneurship, South Africans have found it easier to take control of their own living standards.

Because of growing employment and entrepreneurship, the lower end of the middle class is expanding at an exponential rate – a trend that can best be seen in the rise in consumer spending and savings levels over the past decade. It is estimated that the middle class has doubled in size since 2020 and that it will double again over the decade to 2040. At that point, in 2040, it is expected that the black middle class will be four to five times the size of the white middle class.

Tensions around race are dissipating as living standards improve. Where there are isolated incidents of racial incitement and provocation, these fail to gain the traction they would have had a decade previously, when it appeared as if South Africa risked falling into a debilitating cycle of racial and ethnic recrimination and fragmentation. In part this is because a great political and media effort has been made to highlight areas of common ground between South Africans and not, as was once the case, to focus on areas of difference. But perhaps in greater part it is because a growing economy is offering more opportunities for people to find work, support their families, and take charge of their own lives. Economic expansion means that a growing proportion of directors of listed companies in South Africa are black – even though there are no fewer white directors. The majority of university graduates are black – not because the white students were ejected but rather because more places became available as new tertiary learning institutions were built. Black buyers in the residential market are purchasing twice as many suburban homes as white buyers. A significant majority of all earned income in South Africa is earned by black people even as white income levels also continue to expand.

Growing economic inclusion is seeing an increase in interracial mixing and socialising. This is no surprise as almost all young professionals would have spent several years of high-quality schooling together in the same schools. They are socialised within a common South African identity and do not carry the racial inhibitions or fears of their parents' generation. It is not remarkable, and does not make any newspaper head-lines, for a black person to lead a highly successful business start-up, just as it is not unusual for a white person to occupy a senior job in government.

The initial rise in the number of middle-income households triggered a concomitant rise in inequality levels. This was to be expected, as not all South Africans could be expected to grow wealthier at the same time. However, as the number of middle-income households continues to expand, it is forecast that inequality levels will decline significantly over the two decades between now and 2050.

Much of the success in overcoming inequality relates to improvements in schooling. Those improvements are the result of policy changes that have allowed parents and communities to take back control of schools from politicians and bureaucrats. As it became apparent that the dire state of schools was hindering South Africa's economic performance, the post-2019 government, under massive popular pressure, sought radical solutions. One was to sell government schools to non-profit groups, churches and private education providers for a nominal amount. Parents can use the education grants they receive, supplemented by their own income, to enrol their children at any school, and the market for education this has created has in turn improved the quality of education – which is subject, at the level of every school, to an annual independent quality audit. This change saw South Africa rapidly climb in international education quality rankings. Its Maths and Science results now rival the best of other emerging markets.

The access to, and quality of, post-school education has also improved. Fifteen years ago universities were scenes of conflict and violence. Buildings were burned, standards were tumbling and the best students (and their parents) were focused on study opportunities overseas. That has changed. The real breakthrough was to get politicians out of universities and to reinforce the autonomy of rectors and vice-chancellors to run their campuses as they see fit. Students enrolling at university today have a choice. They can pay their own fees or choose to study free of charge as long as they agree to paying a slightly higher-than-average income tax rate for the rest of their lives. That extra tax is ring-fenced to finance the next generation of university students. As the quality of learning and teaching at universities has improved, so have the employability and earning potential of university graduates.

There has also been much new privately financed investment in vocational post-school education. An extraordinary number of privately run technical and vocational colleges have been established, and there are significantly more students at these colleges than there are at formal universities. South Africa is thus growing the skills it needs to finance continued industrial expansion. More and more firms are happy to pay the fees of students who will, on graduating, come to work for them. All-round vocational skills demand is rising annually, but South Africa has developed a very effective model to keep up with demand.

South Africa finds itself in the midst of a series of virtuous cycles. Living standards are rising, supported by employment and entrepreneurship. The economy is in turn demanding more and better skills, which are being delivered by greatly improved schools and a growing number of post-school education institutions. Better education is in turn pulling poor households into the middle classes. The only regret is that South Africa did not settle into this pattern 25 years ago – if it had done so, the country would today be a wealthy middle-income society.

Supporting the virtuous economic cycle, road, rail, port and air travel infrastructure has more than kept pace with the demands of a growing economy. The expansion of infrastructure has occurred through a model whereby the government borrows cheaply and finances private providers to design, build and, later, operate and manage the infrastructure in question on behalf of the state. For example, if a water-treatment plant is built, the state outsources the construction according to a competitive bid process and also contracts a private provider to run that plant on its behalf to standards that it sets. The state simply creates the environment wherein the plant can be built and allows the leading experts to run that plant as cost-effectively as possible. Expanded to other areas of infrastructure development, this model explains why crises such as electricity blackouts and water shortages have not occurred for many years. The appalling corruption scandals are also a thing of the past – a distant throwback to a time when a corrupt and powerful state followed a destructive ideology that prevented South Africans themselves from taking the lead to exploit the full potential of their country.

Another issue that is disappearing off the agenda is the fear of violent crime. South Africa's murder rate has fallen by half over the past decade, and robbery and most other violent crime rates have reached record lows year after year. Policing policy has changed over the past decade. No longer do most South Africans have to rely on one central and often unaccountable police force. Regional and local forces have been introduced that are answerable to local political leadership structures and communities. Local police chiefs are elected by the communities they serve at the same time as local government elections. This change alone is responsible for South Africa's plummeting crime rates. Politicians have got out of the way. Because communities elect their police chiefs, police managers are professional police officers, selected on merit and answerable to their communities. They are not cadres or political appointees who spend more time playing politics than fighting crime. Civilian involvement in policing has also increased through neighbourhood watch schemes that work closely with private security providers and have augmented the efforts of the police. In addition, the police now attract some of the best and brightest South African graduates – and policing has become a career that people can be proud of.

Young South Africans are the greatest beneficiaries of the virtuous cycles that have positioned South Africa as the leading emerging market in Africa. There was a time when young people were seen as a threat to the future – a destructive influence. For much of South Africa's first three decades as a democracy, the youth unemployment rate was close to 50%. That rate has fallen by half over the past decade and is expected to fall by half again over the next decade.

Better schools, more post-school education opportunities and higher labour-market absorption rates explain much of the turnaround in the fortunes of young people. However, a fourth factor, entrepreneurship, is the most important. The majority of jobs occupied by young people are in small start-up firms or one-person operations – often called work-preneurs. South Africa is spurring a new breed of ambitious, risk-taking young entrepreneur. This is not someone who 'demands' to be 'given' a job. That attitude has disappeared. Nor is this someone who will work for one big company for the rest of his or her life. Rather, the quint-essential young South African is someone who has assembled a unique set of skills and works extremely hard to make those available to a range of clients. This young entrepreneurial class provides the foundation for the rapid growth South Africa has seen in the middle class.

To retain and cater to such a growing middle class, South Africa has had to increase significantly the size and quality of its healthcare services. It did this by adopting a healthcare model similar to that used to turn the education system around. Private providers were asked to tender to run former public clinics and hospitals. Voucher financing and increased household expenditure have allowed more households to qualify for health insurance products that they can use to access better healthcare. The growth in the size of the healthcare market has allowed overall costs to be moderated while creating new opportunities for young health-care professionals and specialists. South Africa has retained its reputa-tion as a world-class private healthcare leader and has found a way to extend that reputation into the public healthcare sector.

Because of improved education and healthcare, expanding infrastruc-ture and an aggressive entrepreneurial culture, South Africa is one of the world's fastest-growing emerging markets. Over the past decade, economic growth rates have risen from near 0% to beyond 6%. This means that the size of the economy is doubling every twelve years. Interest rates have fallen and the budget deficit has been reduced to 3% of GDP even as expenditure on infrastructure and social development has in-creased. The rand has returned to purchasing-power parity levels. The effect of higher levels of growth can be read in real GDP per capita num-bers, which are growing at their fastest rate since the 1950s and 1960s, when South Africa last recorded sustained levels of economic growth at today's rates. As it did for white people 70 or 80 years ago, these levels of growth are making possible the expansion of South Africa's much-celebrated black middle class.

The economy received a further boost from the series of credit-rating upgrades that the country received. This has allowed policy-makers to provide relatively cheap financing to the private sector to deliver the new rail, port, road and aviation infrastructure. To visitors, the country appears as a giant building site, as existing infrastructure is upgraded and new infrastructure is developed. South Africa boasts some of the best roads, ports and airports of all emerging markets – and South Africans are doing the building themselves, unlike the model in much of the rest of Africa, where foreign, often Chinese, contractors are financing and building infrastructure, giving them a great degree of influence over politicians in those countries.

As certainty around policy-making and improved economic performance crystallised, so South Africa came to attract extensive new fixed investment in areas from agriculture to mining, services and manufacturing. The structure of the economy is no longer skewed in favour of the high-tech services industry. Investment in primary and secondary sectors has been crucial to creating the jobs that poor households are relying on to grow out of poverty. South Africa is a major export hub into the rest of Africa and has developed a real degree of export competitiveness – not through slashing wages or reducing protections on offer to workers, but through increasing skills. Nor has this industrial investment and development had to be lured into the country through promises of subsidies and tax breaks. Sub-Saharan Africa is the world's fastest-growing region and is set to become its most exciting new consumer goods market. Global companies want to take advantage of that market, and South Africa has done very well to position itself as the most attractive African investment gateway.

Because crime and corruption levels have fallen and economic growth turned so sharply upwards, what used to be a skills outflow has reversed and sensible new immigration policies make it easy to import skilled professional people into South Africa to augment rising domestic demand. Gone is the idea that foreigners 'steal' resources from South Africans. At the lower end of the skills spectrum, it is forecast that as South Africa's skills and earnings base increases, it may be necessary to import workers from other African countries to provide the unskilled labour that South Africa's infrastructure development and industrial expansion will demand over the next decade.

South Africa is therefore strongly aligned with economic growth trends across the continent. This is the African century and African economies are the new Asian Tiger economies. However, many of them are managed under more dictatorial systems of government – systems in which state planners force unpopular economic reforms onto citizens. South Africa is one of very few exceptions in which, as a democracy, the government has a popular mandate to drive reforms.

None of this could have been achieved in the environment of ideological confusion and policy turmoil that reached its apex between 2014 and 2019. That was an era of rampant corruption in which growth levels and living standards fell sharply as a predatory elite sought to force a divisive and authoritarian agenda on the country – and almost succeeded. The looting and counterproductive economic policy came at a price. Protest levels escalated sharply as living standards fell and poor people found it even more difficult to find work. The government ran out of money to increase social grants at the rate of inflation. Poor students were told that there was no money to send them to university. Health and education programmes had to be scaled back. But there was always money for corrupt tenders and nuclear deals and to bail out failing and corrupt state-owned companies and pay a vast new army of rude and idle civil servants. The government and the ANC had become completely distanced from the people of South Africa.

The consequences started to become clear in 2016 when the ANC saw its support level fall to just 54% in local elections – a continuation of a trend of declining support levels that had actually started a decade earlier after the party reached its highest-ever support level of almost 70%

in the 2004 national elections. Early speculation was that the party could lose the 2019 national elections. The prospects of defeat strengthened the internal resolve of a reformist element within the party to stand up to the corruption and destructive economic policies of their leftist and traditionalist colleagues.

Opinion polls conducted in the build-up to the 2019 elections showed that the ANC was almost certain to lose its national majority. The reformists cleverly employed the prospects of political defeat to entrench their position within the ANC and belatedly force a series of reforms – mainly creating some space for private investors to inject some growth and job creation into the economy. The initial moves towards education and healthcare policy reform were implemented. All the while these reforms were bringing the ruling-party moderates closer to the policy positions of the DA. Despite improved economic performance, the negative political momentum that had attached to the ANC was too great and it saw its support levels slip to below 50% in 2019.

Anticipating an electoral defeat as early as 2019, the ANC's reformist leaders had quietly entered into off-the-record discussions with the leadership of the DA. The DA wanted to remove itself from the unstable and unpopular 'coalition' it had entered into with the EFF three years earlier. The ANC leaders did not want to be forced into a coalition with the EFF. Those discussions culminated in a deal that the DA and the ANC would look to co-operate in more areas of policy, regardless of the election result.

The compromises that were forced by the DA and the ANC having to agree on national policy positions over the past decade have brought about a change in the dominant ideology of the government. It was understood that the state alone could not possibly meet the expectations of South Africans for education, healthcare and employment. It had neither the financial resources nor the human capacity. Continuing with a model of state-led economic development would simply turn public opinion against the emerging new coalition and strengthen the radicals. That emerging coalition therefore saw the merit in giving ordinary people, and the private sector, far greater responsibility to improve their own lives and to take the lead in turning the economy around. The role of the state would be restricted to supporting those efforts and ensuring that the requisite infrastructure, security and civil service efficiency were in place.

Policy around property rights is the best example of how the ideological outlook of the government has improved. The state is no longer seeking ways to dispossess people and businesses of their assets and property. There is no talk of nationalisation or land seizures. Rather, steps have been taken to extend property rights. Investment treaties have been renegotiated to improve property rights protections. Land reform policy, once ground zero of the property rights conflict, has been adjusted to provide financing for emerging farmers to buy their own businesses and receive title to the land they farm. Title has been expanded into the former homelands. Urban mayors present title deeds to homes and properties in urban areas that were previously in the hands of the state.

The securing of property rights was in turn necessary to obtain improved investment inflows and therefore economic growth – another example of a virtuous cycle at work in South Africa. Economic growth has become the single most important focus of government policy. Policies that stand in the way of growth have been removed from the statute books. It is understood that only by creating new wealth can South Africa possibly meet the expectations of its people. Policies that sought to redistribute existing wealth would have the effect of carving up an ever-diminishing pie and could never meet those expectations.

As the economy rebounded, not only the number of jobs but also the level and quality of jobs have increased. People who have remained in employment for more than a few years find that their income levels are increasing – not because of minimum wage laws or other state-enforced dictates – but because they are learning skills and thereby developing stronger bargaining positions with employers.

What had in the run-up to 2019 been a tide of rising popular embitterment changed as the economic prospects of the country improved. In 2019 just 30% of South Africans felt confident about their future in the country. Polls run before last year's 2029 election showed that this had more than doubled to 70%. The once-frightening climate of heightened racial and ethnic animosity has dissipated. This should come as no surprise, as South Africa has always shown a correlation between the economic performance of households and attitudes towards the country, political parties and the future. In eras of weak economic performance tensions increased, whereas in eras of better performance they dissipated.

As perceptions and social relations improved, South Africans began to emerge from their self-imposed internal exile in race- and class-denominated enclaves. Rights to cultural and language determination exist comfortably alongside a common South African identity. Much of the credit for this belongs to the media and civil society, which have played a critically important role in promoting better relations between South Africans. That tensions were dissipating slowed the growth of radical socialist parties and extremist racial nationalist movements on both the left and right of the political spectrum. Parties that once campaigned on platforms of hate and division are disappearing, and in 2029 the collective post-2019 DA–ANC coalition was returned to power with almost 70% of the vote.

There was a time when it seemed as if some newspapers and activist groups revelled in the worst that South Africa had to offer. Even petty cases of racial conflict were elevated to front-page headline status. The millions of South Africans who wanted to work together, despite tough circumstances, were barely mentioned at all. This was an era in which the country celebrated its worst and derided its best. Today, all that seems to belong to an era very far away – one that it is difficult to believe could ever have existed at all.

Chapter 12: Through a glass, darkly

What is left to do is only to say which of the four scenarios is likely to pan out in South Africa. Let us recap what we know.

We know that relatively small changes to the present conditions of a country or economy are likely to trigger dramatic future shifts – the butterfly effect applied to politics and economics. The example of Mohamed Bouazizi in Tunisia is a particularly stark case study of this phenomenon. The odds of profound change are heightened when the people in that country or economy become dissatisfied with their present circumstances. Our own history is a case in point of how economic slowdowns trigger major political shifts. That was the case in the aftermath of the Anglo-Boer War, with Smuts's defeat in the election of 1948, and again in the 1980s – the first, second and third transitions. The third of these transitions, what is often referred to as *the* transition, occurred in the decade after real GDP per head had hit its all-time peak of just over R50,000 in 1981 – a function of the high growth rates the country had sustained throughout the 1950s and 1960s and into the increasingly politically volatile 1970s. By the 1980s, however, despite a record-high gold price at a time when South Africa was the world's biggest gold producer, the contradictions upon which the apartheid system rested – a growing economy and rising living standards matched with the political exclusion of the majority of the population – began to unravel. In real terms, South Africans spent the 1980s and the first three years of the 1990s becoming poorer, a trend that the once-powerful National Party realised it was powerless to withstand, forcing its capitulation.

Elected to office with 63% of the vote in 1994, the ANC immediately set about facing up to the economic wreckage it had inherited. It was here, in its initial economic policies, that it had its greatest successes.

GDP growth rates recovered to average over 3% between 1994 and 2007. For four of those years, between 2004 and 2007, growth rates averaged upwards of 5%. That was a crucial period since, when growth breached the 5% level, the unemployment rate began to fall quickly and popular confidence in the future peaked.

Improving economic conditions allowed for a commensurate improvement in living standards. The number of South Africans with a job approximately doubled between 1994 and 2007. The number of families in formal houses more than doubled. For every shack newly erected in the country, more than formal houses were being built. Water and electricity rollout into poor communities demonstrated equally impressive numbers. More than a thousand households were being connected to electricity daily. The black middle class grew to rival the size of the white middle class. A quite remarkable transformation occurred in the higher education sector. Black South Africans became the majority buyers of homes in what had formerly been white suburbia. The proportion of children under the age of five who were malnourished fell from roughly 14% to between 4% and 5% of children in that age bracket.

Life was getting better in South Africa and real progress was being made in escaping its apartheid past. The economic and social progress was essential to consolidating the ANC's popular mandate – and for many years after 1994 it did not seem to matter much that no credible political rival existed. By the time of the national elections of 2004, the ANC received a larger majority than when Nelson Mandela had led the party in the elections of 1994.

It was not to last.

In December 2007 everything changed. The ANC held a conference at which it elected a new set of leaders. To the surprise of many, although not to analysts at the IRR, Thabo Mbeki, who had served as leader of the ANC as well as President of South Africa, and who had been central to the economic policy-making of the party and the government, was removed as ANC leader.

In dispensing with Mbeki, the ANC dispensed with more than the man. It also rejected much of the pragmatism of his economic policies. The South African Communist Party and COSATU, both of which had been central to the dismissal of Mbeki, became increasingly prominent in policy-making. Following the 2009 national election, a number of key economic portfolios in the cabinet were in the hands of leftists and communists. They quickly set about dismantling the policy infrastructure of the 1994–2007 era and replaced it with a concept they called 'the developmental state'. Leaks from cabinet meetings suggest that animated ideological debates took place about what such a state would entail – mostly concluding with ideological dogma about nationalisation and talk of the expropriation of various industries.

Policy soon began to reflect that dogma. Proposals were made to nationalise mines and banks. A cabinet minister spoke of the need to destroy the capitalist system. A deputy minister accused foreign investors of looting the country. Another member of the cabinet proposed putting a ceiling on all private sector management salaries until economic equality had been attained (appearing oblivious to the consequences for tax revenue). Labour laws were tightened. Firms that failed to meet the state-driven racial targets were publicly shamed. It was proposed that the private security industry be nationalised. Proposals were made to nationalise all land in private hands. Laws were passed that diluted protections for foreign investors. An antagonistic line was adopted towards Western capitals and capital. Chávez in Venezuela, Castro in Cuba and Mugabe in Zimbabwe were hailed as role models to be emulated.

That this shift in policy coincided with the global financial crisis and growing risk-aversion to emerging markets greatly exacerbated its impact, as did the commodity price pull-back. At a time of heightened global investor concern, South Africa was sending out the message that it did not value investment and would not protect the rights of investors – whether foreign or domestic.

Domestic policy hostility intersected with challenging global conditions, and economic growth, which had averaged 5% in the four years to 2007, is now flirting with recession. Public debt levels have approximately doubled since 2007. Formal private sector job creation has been effectively stagnant for five to six years. The full range of indicators that are tracked to develop an advance view of the South African economy are not encouraging – from mining and manufacturing production indices to residential property prices, vehicle sales, credit extension and default numbers, business confidence indices, consumer confidence indices, and consumer spending itself. The leading indicator is in its longest slump since the Rubicon speech of 1985. The most telling number of all is that, in real GDP terms, South Africans are again becoming poorer – as they last did in the volatile and very violent 1980s.

The gap that opened between the expectations curve and the rate of economic growth has visited a crisis of rising, but unmet, expectations upon the country. The political consequences are turning out to be as severe as they were in the 1980s when a once-powerful and entrenched administration was dethroned. Waves of protest have shaken the seemingly impregnable political edifice of the ANC and a revolutionary tide laps even at the doors of Luthuli House.

There is no question that the fourth transition is upon us.

From an analyst's perspective, it seems foolish for the ANC government not to appreciate that its political mandate rested in large part on its economic performance. In sacrificing that performance in pursuit of its ideological goals, the ANC did more than any other group to create the forces that now threaten to bring it down. Yet an intransigence born of ideological stubbornness and warring factions within prevents it from acting decisively enough, even at this late stage, to save itself.

Two sets of trends will determine how the fourth transition plays out – the role of the state and whether expectations can be met. On one hand, the state could grow ever more powerful and use that power to force reform or repress dissent. On the other hand, it could wane, either fading into effective insignificance or stepping back, creating the circumstances South Africans need to improve their own lives. At the same time expectations for a better life may be met, or South Africa may become a much poorer society.

Where these trends intersect, four scenarios emerge.

The first is the *Rise of the Right*, where the state grows more powerful and authoritarian and uses that authority to force pragmatic economic policies that take the growth rate back to around 5%. The route towards this future will look something as follows. ANC reformists gain a balance of power in the ruling party over the next eighteen months. They consolidate control of the party at its internal leadership elections in December 2017 and lead the party to contest the 2019 national elections and choose a reformist cabinet. The cabinet moves quickly and firmly to secure property rights, deregulate the labour market, professionalise the sluggish civil service, and employ the private sector as partners on the road to rebuilding the South African economy. Where opposition to the government's reformist agenda is encountered, we expect it to act decisively and at times very harshly to ensure that its reforms are not derailed. Such firm action may extend to the point of undermining civil rights, free speech, the sanctity of the courts, rights to free political association, and the standing of trade unions and other civil society groups. If the reformist agenda is pursued with vigour against the backdrop of a global economic recovery, we anticipate South Africa's debt and interest rates peaking in the period around 2020, before declining to levels last seen around 2006. Economic growth levels that will have averaged below 2% into 2019 will commence a gradual rise, to reach average rates in excess of 5% by 2025 and maintain those levels into 2030. The currency will strengthen back to purchasing-power parity levels by the mid-2020s, while the current account and budget deficits will narrow. In material terms, life for all South Africans will become significantly better, and a combination of improving socio-economic circumstances and the ruthless repression of dissent will stabilise the country.

It is a future in which South Africans would cede some of their political freedoms in exchange for growing prosperity and the promise of stability. Where growing prosperity is achieved, it will resemble the development model that was followed by many of the Asian Tiger economies – albeit with very important differences – and it will become the primary influence in shaping the evolution of high-growth economies across the African continent.

Clem Sunter speaks of flags that we should watch for in order to know which one of a set of scenarios will materialise. To get to *Rise of the Right*, each of the following five flags must be seen to be going up.

Flags	
1	The ANC unites as one behind a reformist leadership.
2	The cabinet introduces a series of firm reforms to labour market policy, secures property rights, and dispenses with current affirmative action and empowerment policies in favour of an empowerment model centred around growth and employment.
3	An immensely impressive and efficient civil service arises.
4	The government quashes any dissent in its tracks.
5	The world experiences a sustained long-term economic recovery and South Africa is well on its way to growth rates of 5%.

This scenario is plausible for South Africa. It is also the model of development that is being pursued with some economic success in Rwanda and Ethiopia. But it is not at this point the most probable scenario, as crippling factionalism matched with dated leftist ideology still have too much of a hold over the leadership of the ANC. Until it breaks free from that hold, the party will not embrace a reformist mandate with sufficient enthusiasm. Then, even if the ideological obstacles can be overcome, the civil service remains too weak, corrupt and inefficient to implement the changes required with the requisite haste and efficiency.

Yet we know that many in the government and the ANC find the model of *Rise of the Right* appealing. They like what they see in Ethiopia and Rwanda and fantasise about 'being like China'. But their attempt to pursue the model may be very dangerous, since, where prosperity is not forthcoming, it is a model that invites a system of rule with impunity from which South Africa may not escape for some considerable time.

Authoritarianism in the absence of successful economic reform will take South Africa into the scenario of the *Tyranny of the Left*. In this future South Africa, the state becomes extremely powerful but uses that power not for reform but to suppress dissent arising out of unmet expectations.

In this future, the leftist factions of South Africa's ruling class remain influential in any political realignment and the ruling party will not develop an effective economic policy agenda while ideological dogma predominates in the cabinet. Growth levels will slip further as investment dries up and South Africa experiences a decade of volatile stagnation – a term we use to describe a society that is making no economic progress as its politics become more volatile. This is quite possibly a future of deep recession and declining living standards. Deficit and debt levels will escalate sharply and economic and industrial output will fall, even as the currency weakens. The rand will slide. Anti-government protest action will escalate sharply and will be met, when not with rubber bullets and arrests, with wild populist promises and hateful racial rhetoric and incitement to terrible violence. Property rights are then likely to be eroded as well as civil liberties, as a rapacious and ideologically stubborn state refuses to reform on policy. Where populism alone is not sufficient to supress dissent, the state will likely unleash terror on its people.

If this future is to happen, the following five flags will be seen going up:

Flags	
1	The ANC unites behind a cruel and corrupt leadership.
2	Redistributionist socialist dogma takes the place of growth-focused reformist policy.
3	Racial tensions are intentionally ratcheted up amid rising levels of violence.
4	An assault is launched against democratic institutions, property rights and critical or dissenting voices.
5	The economy falters between recession and very low rates of growth.

This outcome is probably more likely than the *Rise of the Right*. Our democracy, the Constitution, civil society and the free media are not nearly as strong as some people would like to believe, and could be snuffed out in months. Destroying the economy in the manner implicit in this scenario, while deflecting the blame onto minorities and the private sector, may also buy the ruling party considerable time, but it is unclear whether the state will be able to act with the unity of purpose and the requisite efficiency to pull off such an orchestrated destruction of the country. It will also have to overcome the good sense of South Africa's people and get them to turn against each other to a far greater extent than has been possible to date.

This then opens the way to the third of our scenarios, where the state is too inept to reform but also too inept to maintain a solid grip on power. In *The Break-up* scenario the state weakens as the economy stalls and South Africans gradually drift apart into enclaves. On the basis of trends we are currently experiencing this is the scenario of greatest probability and the one we think South Africans will live through in the years to 2030.

It seems unlikely that the economic and political establishment will unite around a plan that will go far enough to fix the South African economy. A political reformation and general clean-up of corruption and inefficiency within the ANC will not be enough – a fundamental economic reformation is also necessary. All the easy economic levers have been pulled, and such an economic reformation would have to be built around labour-market reform, the guaranteeing of property rights, and a complete reworking of South Africa's empowerment laws. Yet even the DA is not willing to accept the necessity of the third point while some ANC reformers think they can be successful without the second. Even if the plan can be drafted, the state does not have the expertise and efficiency to implement it. Global circumstances are also still against South Africa. Without political reform, the corruption and ineptitude of the civil service will become worse, and without economic reform the government will inevitably run out of money. This will compromise its ability to fund social services and infrastructure development. Economic growth will muddle along at very low levels – dipping into recession in the event of tougher global circumstances while at other times possibly reaching highs of 2% to 3% when global circumstances allow. Inflation and interest rates as well as debt levels will increase. The rand will lose value. Schools, universities and government hospitals will decay and standards will decline. Massive protests will take place, accompanied by high levels of violence and destruction of property. Racial recrimination and rhetoric will increase with occasional spillovers into violence. The state will declare that order must return, but no one will pay it any heed. It will make threats and promises but nothing will come of these. Eventually the ruling party will lose an election, but the coalitions that succeed it will be even more volatile. As the state's authority weakens, other types of organisations will emerge as forms of parallel government. The rule of law will slowly slip away, as will the state's monopoly on the use of force in society. Here and there the lights will be going out and the water will be cut off. Crime, poverty and unemployment will increase, while citizens increasingly give up on the state and withdraw into class, race and ethnic enclaves.

These are the flags that will signal such a future:

Flags	
1	The ANC squabbles with itself even as the walls of Luthuli House start tumbling down.
2	Policy remains contradictory and confusing.
3	Protests increase dramatically and take on repugnant racial and ethnic overtones.
4	People start ignoring the government and the state.
5	Family, friends and communities begin to develop their own plans to look after their own schooling, healthcare, security and other needs.

This is not the worst of outcomes – far from it. It fairly approximates the uncertainty and under-performance of the past couple of years. If you are in one of the more upmarket enclaves and are well hedged, your standard of living may be very good. From schooling and healthcare to security and infrastructure, you will be largely on your own. Many South Africans are already much further down that road than they realise. Libertarians may even welcome this scenario as the highest form of human freedom. But if you are trapped in a rural backwater, under the control of a corrupt traditional leader or in some abysmal urban slum, your life will be very hard indeed, with no upside prospects.

If this is not to be our future, then the only option left is the fourth scenario, the *Rise of the Rainbow*, which is without question South Africa's most positive outcome. It would preserve and strengthen democracy as a means of securing an economic recovery. It will see the state not so much weaken and decay but rather step back and allow the private sector to take the lead in meeting the popular expectations of South Africans.

The only plausible route to that future is either through an outright DA political victory in 2019 or alternatively a DA–ANC coalition, and for this reason it cannot be our most probable outcome at this time. Such a coalition would see the best of the DA and the better components of the ANC come together around a reformist agenda. The state would become smaller and much more efficient – freeing the economy and relying on the private sector to deliver services. Investment-driven economic growth would pick up to over 5%. Debt and deficit levels would fall. The unemployment rate would fall rapidly. Large numbers of entrepreneurs will absorb the unemployed. Excellent schools, universities and hospitals will be readily available. South Africa would become a safer country for all of its citizens. Common prosperity would unite South Africa's people.

In this more hopeful case, you will see each of the following five flags being raised:

Flags	
1	The ANC and the DA come together around the importance of sensible economic reforms to labour laws, the importance of property rights, and the need for effective empowerment policies.
2	That coming together translates into a turn in government policy that seeks out private sector investment to take the lead in rebuilding South Africa.
3	The policy is effectively implemented.
4	Racial and social tensions are transitioned into a new mood of unity and common purpose.
5	The global economy recovers and South Africa is well on its way to growth rates of 5%.

Late in the day as it is, this outcome is still within our reach. There are good people in both the DA and the ANC who would be open to this outcome. But they will need enormous support in South Africa's battle of ideas if they are to prevail. They will also need a global recovery to underpin their efforts. Even more daunting is the fact that they will have to overcome their own internal political constraints to find each other. As little of this holds true for the immediate present, *The Break-up* must remain the scenario that is the most likely to prevail.

I regret that the scenario on which we have settled is not the *Rise of the Rainbow*, but our analysis must be guided by a realistic appraisal of the facts – and not merely hopes and fears or the pressures of political correctness. While it has regrettably become difficult to offer a frank and honest as well as broadly positive assessment of where South Africa is headed, it also serves no purpose to play down the real threats to our future, the ineptitude of the current government, and the devastating consequences of its racial and ideological fixations. There can be little doubt that past reluctance to face up to those hard truths, a function of South Africa's obsessive and crippling political correctness, contributed to getting the country into its current political and economic predicament.

Never forget that it is a mistake to fixate on just one of the scenarios to the point of dispensing with the others. Small changes in the present conditions of complex systems will bring about great shifts in their future circumstances. Each scenario is plausible and, if circumstances change, be prepared to shift your thinking on where South Africa is headed. There is, however, not a fifth scenario, and South Africa's future will fall within one of the four that appear in this book.

Watch the flags very closely, have access to good information, and always be properly briefed so that nothing can happen in a future South Africa that takes you by surprise. Read the environment closely, and you, your business and your family will have significant advance warning to plan and hedge for any eventuality. That alone puts you in a very strong position regardless of South Africa's trajectory. There is no excuse to say, 'We did not see it coming.'

Thriving in the type of country South Africa is likely to become over the next decade and a bit will require a great degree of independence and community resilience. Don't expect that the state will do much for you; be aware that more often than not it will get in your way. Those who wait for the government to provide for them will be disappointed. Those who turn in anger on their fellow citizens will simply be placing a better future for themselves further out of reach.

Communities that work together, despite the state, and across lines of race, class and ethnicity may come to do quite well. If we are fortunate enough, this realisation may expand to bring forth great volumes of the hope, faith and charity that continue to exist within ordinary South Africans – and upon which our country may in future decades yet reach its extraordinary potential.

Acknowledgements

I am indebted to a great many people who all played a direct or indirect role in the publication of this book. I am grateful to Annie Olivier for asking me on behalf of Tafelberg to write the first book of this series, and to Maryna Lamprecht for commissioning this second book. Professor André Duvenhage of North West University supervised the doctoral thesis that developed the methodology upon which this series is based. I am grateful to my IRR colleagues, including my ever-patient assistant Susi Eusman, Professor Jonathan Jansen, Theo Coggin, Kerwin Lebone, Thuthukani Ndebele, Dr Anthea Jeffery, John Kane-Berman, Carol Archibald, Tamara Dimant, Gwen Ngwenya, and others too many to mention, for their collective support over many years. Scenario experts Clem Sunter and Louis van der Merwe have both been very generous in their support and advice. I am grateful to Dawie Roodt, Ian Cruickshanks, John Loos, Willemien Klinger, Laureen Bertin, and Russell Martin for advising on and improving the manuscript.

FRANS CRONJE
Johannesburg

Index

FRANS CRONJE is a scenario planner and the CEO of South Africa's leading policy think tank, the IRR. In 2007, he established its Centre for Risk Analysis, which advises company boards, strategic planning teams and policy-makers on short-, medium- and long-term strategic decisions for South Africa. He has advised and presented scenarios to the bulk of South Africa's major foreign and domestic investors as well as government agencies and several foreign governments. His first book, *A Time Traveller's Guide to Our Next Ten Years,* was published in 2014.

Cronje was educated at St John's College in Houghton and Wits University, and holds a PhD in scenario planning from North-West University. Prior to joining the IRR, he lived and worked in the United States of America and completed a year-long expedition from Cape Town to Cairo.

To learn more about the Time Traveller's scenarios visit www.frans-cronje.com.